Desmond O'Donnell is a member of the Oblate community of which he has been General Counsellor for twelve years. He conducts retreats and lectures on matters psycho-spiritual internationally. He is a registered psychologist resident in Dublin.

Maureen Mohen is a Sister of Mercy belonging to the Perth Congregation, Western Australia. A musician and teacher, she has produced a number of worship resources, and is now involved in full-time pastoral work.

Praying the Good News

A Rich Resource of Psalmed Prayers
from the New Testament

DESMOND O'DONNELL
MAUREEN MOHEN

 Fount
An Imprint of HarperCollins*Publishers*

Fount is an Imprint of
HarperCollins*Religious*
Part of HarperCollins*Publishers*
77–85 Fulham Palace Road, London W6 8JB

First published in Great Britain in 1998 by Fount

10 9 8 7 6 5 4 3 2 1

Copyright © 1998 Desmond O'Donnell and Maureen Mohen

Desmond O'Donnell and Maureen Mohen assert the moral right
to be identified as the authors of this work

A catalogue record for this book
is available from the British Library

ISBN 0 00 628051 X

Printed and bound in Great Britain by
Caledonian International Book Manufacturing Ltd, Glasgow

All Christian living is founded on prayer and that prayer has a particular focus when it is grounded in Holy Scripture. Because prayer is an encounter with God it is something that transcends denominational boundaries and I am sure that *Praying the Good News* will be a useful resource for all Christians, helping them to encounter the New Testament in new and creative ways. I warmly commend it.

George Carey, Archbishop of Canterbury

Prayer is so important. Most of us need help with it. I believe that this book will give great help to a number of people and especially because it is based on the Scriptures.

Cardinal Basil Hume

I warmly recommend this book of scriptural prayers to readers who have a desire to make the Word of God an integral part of their prayer life. This is a collection of prayers which are rich in scriptural content, containing as they do many themes from the New Testament as well as using a multitude of New Testament texts. A particularly useful feature of the book is the thematic list of contents which gives easy reference to prayers which may be helpful at specific moments in our lives.

Sean Brady, Archbishop of Armagh

People of faith are called to pilgrimage. In order to journey well prayer is vital. In an increasingly busy world often this can be difficult. This book of prayer provides food for the journey, signposts along the way, and a rich mine of encouragement for those who travel. Praying the Word in this way leads the pilgrim deeper into the heart of God, and provides the equipment necessary to be fully present in and to his world.

Rev Ruth Patterson, Presbyterian Minister, Belfast
Director of Restoration Ministries

Praying the Good News is a different kind of prayer book. Totally scriptural, it is direct, deep and full of feeling but devoid of sentimentality. It will help the Spirit to pray through us 'according to the will of God' (Rom 8:27).

Ronald Rolheiser

The language of the New Testament is so familiar that it is easy to take it for granted and let it wash over us. By using an ancient and well-tried method, *Praying the Good News* presents us with a fresh and valuable perspective that makes it possible to think again about the familiar words and come closer to what they mean.

Professor David Crystal,
Editor of *The Cambridge Encyclopedia*

Contents

Introduction

This book of prayer is the fruit of many years journeying with our own spirits, with others on retreats and through spiritual guidance – Maureen as a teacher and catechist; myself as a priest and spiritual guide.

As a psychologist I also developed a strong interest in the point of intersection and mode of interaction between human development and faith. My clinical experience confirms the value of prayer for growth and for healing. The scriptural word received in faith and reflected on – like any word spoken and heard in love – is always a healing, growth-giving experience.

Because of my professional interest in the value of encouragement for personal growth and healing, I was excited to find the word *parakaleo*(n) and *paraklesis* (v) thirty-four times in the New Testament. When I put all these references together, I found that I had material for a beautiful prayer before me. And so, 'Encouragement' became the first prayer theme for this book. During a sabbatical in Jerusalem I researched ninety-nine other themes.

Maureen, with her long experience, deep prayerfulness and giftedness in the use of music and rhythm for catechetical purposes, was able to express these texts in psalm-prayers as they now appear.

The authors of the Old Testament Psalms clearly prayed from their own experience – loved by God, love of God, need of God, in praise and petition, in repentance and thanksgiving. The value of praying from one's present experience is well recognized, and so I chose themes which express a wide variety of human needs and feelings. A glance at the contents list will make an appropriate choice easy at any time.

If you think yourself a beginner in prayer, where better to begin than from your present experience expressed in the words of God chosen from these themes? This might be especially beneficial for young adults struggling with their personal faith in Christian schools.

If you have always been a prayerful person, the use of these psalm-prayers, slowly reflected upon, will deepen your experience of God. Jesus said 'If you make my word your home, you will indeed be my *disciples*' (John 8:31). The word of God used in prayer will increasingly *discipline* us into true discipleship.

We offer you the references for each verse, so that you can go to the context, in order to relish the words more deeply. While the Psalms you may have recited for many years express only hope for the Redeemer and for resurrection, these prayers from the New Testament celebrate their arrival. Hence we can pray with a deep gratitude and a growing awareness of what it means to be truly New Testament people.

Today, more and more small groups of Christians – even those outside official church membership – are coming together to pray. If you belong to one of these groups, you will find this book very useful for shared scripture-based prayer. Church and group leaders will also find it helpful to build a talk or a retreat around one theme and then have their group pray the chosen theme together.

Christian liturgies such as baptisms, weddings, eucharists and reconciliation services can be enhanced by the use of these New Testament prayers. So too can family celebrations and special prayer-moments for Mother's Day, Father's Day, birthdays or school assemblies.

Maureen and I wish to express our thanks to our communities which gave us the time and encouragement to put this book of prayer together. We also thank my cousin Evin, whose deep sense of the beautiful, expressed in continual advice as she typed and improved the text, made her contribution so important. Our thanks also to Elizabeth Devine who brought us together on this project, and most of all to God who inspired it.

How to Use This Book

The guiding principle should be flexibility. Each prayer has a different theme, and we devote about ten verses, thoughts, or insights, to exploring each theme. The themes can of course be read in any sequence, and the same point applies to the way you read the individual verses.

These verses differ greatly in language, coming as they do from different writers and from different parts of the New Testament. Some are poetic in their rhythm and style, some are prosaic. Do not read them in a rush. Each one is self-contained, and deserves individual contemplation. Give each a pause, a moment for reflection.

Although we have put the verses in an order which, to our mind, expresses one way of developing the theme, there are many other possible sequences. You should certainly not feel it necessary to read each prayer from 'top to bottom'. Let your eye fall on them as it will, allowing the different nuances and emphases to interact, and this will deepen your appreciation of the theme as a whole.

1.   *Beatitudes (Luke)*

God, help us to own that the poor are blessed;
the kingdom of heaven is theirs.
~

Satisfy us, as we hunger and thirst
for justice and peace in our world.
~

You bless us in our weeping and in our mourning.
You turn our tears into laughter.
~

And blessed are we when reviled and hated,
defamed on account of Jesus.
~

Gladden our hearts that we may rejoice.
Our reward is great in heaven.
~

Empty our lives, God, of worldly riches.
We await your own consolation.
~

Temper our greed, our desire for more.
Remind us that some have nothing.
~

And gentle our laughing – our self-centred fun,
mindful of those who weep.
~

Let us never depend on human appraisal.
It is you, God, who search the heart.

~

Make us sincere, authentic and true.
We want to be Jesus' disciples.

REFERENCES
Luke 6:20–26

2. *Beatitudes (Matthew)*

Draw us, God, into poorness of spirit
as we journey to the heavenly kingdom.
~

Make holy our mourning for those in distress.
May we taste your Spirit's comforting.
~

In gentleness let us open our hearts
to whatever your goodness has planned.
~

As we hunger and thirst for a world that is just,
give us the fullness Christ promised.
~

In mercy amid outgoing kindness of heart,
we too will receive your mercy.
~

Cleanse our hearts from all ungodliness
so that we may see you, our God.
~

As bearers of peace, embracing all,
your very own children shall we be.
~

And when faith brings suffering into our lives,
we know it is the road to the kingdom.
~

In times of trial, when falsely accused,
fill us with joy and gladness.

~

Like the prophets before us, we cling to your promise
– fullness of joy in your presence.

REFERENCE
Matt. 5:3–12

3. *Blessing*

'Blessed be the God and Father of our Lord Jesus Christ,
who has blessed us with every spiritual blessing,
in the heavenly places, in Christ.'[1]

~

Blessed be the God of mercies, the God of all consolation.
In all our afflictions, we are consoled.
May we share this blessing with others.[2]

~

With grateful hearts, let us sing psalms and hymns
and spiritual songs to our God, for within us is dwelling
    the word of Christ.
May we know its richness in depth.[3]

~

Mould our hearts into love for our enemies,
for those who curse us, a blessing.
Bring us to offering goodness for hate
and praying for those who abuse us.[4]

~

The cup of blessing that we bless
and the bread that was blessed and broken
became the body and blood of Christ.
Transform us, God, into blessing.[5]

~

God, you give us every blessing in abundance.
There is always enough of everything.
Take all reluctance out of our lives.
Make us cheerful in giving.[6]

~

Give us the faith of Abraham who believed
and went without knowing.
Gift us with the blessing of those who believe.
Bless all families of the earth.[7]

~

Worthy is the Lamb that was slaughtered
to receive power and wealth,
wisdom and might and honour,
glory and blessing forever.[8]

~

Let us not change the truth for a lie
to worship and serve the creature
but strengthen our faithfulness to you our creator
who is blessed forever. Amen.[9]

REFERENCES
1) Eph. 1:3
2) 2 Cor. 1:3, 4
3) Col. 3:16
4) Luke 6:27, 28
5) 1 Cor. 10:16
6) 2 Cor. 9:7, 8
7) Heb. 11:8, 9
8) Rev. 5:11–13
9) Rom. 1:25

4.   *The Body*

'And the Word was made flesh' – a body like ours.[1]

~

In Christ dwells bodily the whole fullness of deity.[2]

~

We know, God, that within us your own spirit dwells.
Your temple is holy and we are that temple.[3]

~

We are not our own; we have been bought at a price.
Yours the gift we carry; we glorify you in our body.[4]

~

Let not sin dominate our bodies
making them instruments of wickedness.
But enable the presenting of our bodies to you
as instruments of righteousness.[5]

~

Worrying not about food and clothes
– more worth our life, our body.
You know, God, that we need these things.
Deepen our trust in you.[6]

~

Keep blameless our spirit, soul and body
at the coming of Jesus Christ
– the one who calls, the faithful one.
You will do this for us.[7]

~

Approaching the sanctuary, our body
with true heart and faith,
sprinkled clean from an evil conscience,
our bodies washed in water pure.[8]

～

Fill us with longing for the resurrection of the dead,
when what is sown in weakness is raised in power
and imperishability and immortality are ours.[9]

～

Now, as always, whether by life or death,
may Christ be exalted in our body.[10]

REFERENCES
1) John 1:14   2) Col. 2:9
3) 1 Cor. 3:16, 17   4) 1 Cor. 6:19, 20
5) Rom. 6:12, 13   6) Luke 12:22–31
7) 1 Thess. 5:23   8) Heb. 10:22
9) 1 Cor. 15:42–54   10) Phil. 1:20

5. *Celebration*

Rejoice in your God always and again I say rejoice!
Let your gentleness be known to everyone
for God is near.[1]
~

Rejoice ever and always;
unceasing be your prayer,[2]
asking and receiving,
completing your joy.[3]
~

Work for joy with one another,
standing firmly in the faith,[4]
rejoicing even when hated –
in heaven your reward is great.[5]
~

Rejoice in the truth, for such is love,[6]
suffering patiently, faithful in prayer,
in hope rejoicing as one.[7]
~

In the spirit of God rejoice,
celebrating with thanksgiving,
for you, God's little ones,
have been shown the mysteries of the Kingdom.[8]
~

Rejoice and be glad in love
for the Father is greater than I am
and his Spirit, the Advocate he will send.[9]

~

With you, I share all this
that you may know my joy,
a joy unbounded – complete.[10]

REFERENCES
1) Phil. 4:4
2) 1 Thess. 5:16, 17
3) John 16:24
4) 2 Cor. 1:24
5) Luke 6:22, 23
6) 1 Cor. 13:6
7) Rom. 12:12–14
8) Luke 10:21
9) John 14:28
10) John 15:11

6. Christ – His Authority

God, who can resist your will;
who are we humans to argue with you?
Will what is moulded say to the one who moulds –
why have you made me like this?
Has the potter no right over the clay
to make something for ordinary use, something
    for special?[1]

~

You have granted your Son to have life in himself
and given him authority to execute judgement
because he is the Son of Man.[2]

~

For now have come the salvation
and the power and the kingdom that is your own
and the authority of your Messiah.[3]

~

To Jesus has been given all authority in heaven and
    on earth.[4]
He has authority over all people, all things.[5]

~

His the authority that offers forgiveness,
that casts the demons out,
that teaches as no other has taught,
that executes judgement justly.[6]

To all who receive him, who believe in his name,
he gives in abundance the gift of life,
the power to become God's children.[7]

REFERENCES
1) Rom. 9:19–21
3) Rev. 12:10
5) John 17:2
7) John 1:12; 10:10

2) John 5:26, 27
4) Matt. 28:18
6) Mark 2:10; 3:14, 15;
    Matt. 7:29; John 5:30

7. *Christ – Human*

'And the Word was made flesh and lived among us.'[1]
God, your Son Jesus emptied himself,
taking the form of a slave
and being born in human likeness.[2]

~

Conceived and born of a virgin,
wrapped in bands of cloth,
laid in a manger, no place at the inn,
Christ human, one of us.[3]

~

Like us in every respect, yet sinless
and tested by what he suffered,
he is our merciful and faithful high priest,
able to atone for all our sins
and to help those being tested.[4]

~

Knowing that Jesus can sympathize with our weaknesses
and that mercy and grace are there for the asking,
let us turn to him in our every need
and come to the throne of grace.[5]

~

You deal with us gently, Jesus,
with the ignorance and the waywardness that are ours.[6]
You weep with us over our sinful world
tears of tenderness and compassion.[7]

You knew tiredness as you sat by the well[8]
and grieved over hardness of heart,[9]
experienced hunger from weeks in the desert[10]
and had nowhere to lay your head.[11]

~

You joined in the banquet prepared by Levi[12]
and Cana's wedding feast.[13]
You loved your visits to Martha and Mary[14]
and children you gently caressed.[15]

~

Bring us to understand clearly, God,
that all life's moments are sacred,
whether joyous or sad,
whether painful or glad,
all are experienced in Jesus.[16]

REFERENCES
1) John 1:14
2) Phil. 2:5–7
3) Luke 1:31; 2:6, 7
4) Heb. 2:16–18
5) Heb. 4:15, 16
6) Heb. 5:2
7) Luke 19:41
8) John 4:6
9) Mark 2:5–8
10) Luke 4:1, 2
11) Luke 9:58
12) Luke 5:29
13) John 2:1, 2
14) John 11:5
15) Mark 9:36
16) Rom. 8:28; 12:15

8. *Christ – Icon of God*

And the Word became flesh; his glory was seen
– the glory of the Father's only Son.[1]

~

In Christ was life and that life was the light of all people.
The true light which enlightens everyone
was coming into the world.[2]

~

Sent by God, he spoke the words of God.
He alone had seen the Father
and to him without measure, the Spirit was given.[3]

~

He is the way, the truth and the life.
Through him all come to the Father.[4]

~

Knowing Jesus means knowing the Father
and seeing Jesus is seeing the Father too.[5]

~

Jesus spoke as the Father instructed,
knowing that the One who sent him is true.[6]

~

The prayer of Christ – that all may be one –
enabled belief in the One who sent him.[7]

~

In answer to Jesus, a voice came from heaven
– I have glorified my name and will do so again.[8]

~

The Father dwells in me, said Jesus
and within the Father I also dwell.[9]

~

What was heard and seen by human eye,
looked at and touched by human hands
– the Word of life revealed to the world
Christ, icon of God.[10]

REFERENCES
1) John 1:14
3) John 3:32–34
5) John 14:7–9
7) John 17:21
9) John 14:9, 10

2) John 1:4–9
4) John 14:6
6) John 8:28; 7:28, 29
8) John 12:27, 28
10) John 1:1, 2

9. Christ – King

God, the blessed and only Sovereign,
King of kings and Lord of lords,
alone, immortal, dwelling in light unapproachable,
no one has ever seen you,
no one can behold you;
to you be honour and eternal dominion.[1]
~
Your Son Jesus, Son of the Most High,
receives the throne of his ancestor David,
reigning over the house of Jacob forever.
His kingdom – unceasing.[2]
~
Jesus, remember us; make us part of your kingdom,[3]
a kingdom – not of this world,
a kingdom – not from here.[4]
~
Mould us into sinlessness, Jesus,
that we may inherit the kingdom,[5]
where the righteous will shine, bright as the sun,[6]
when your kingdom comes with power.[7]
~
Your kingdom, like the mustard seed
sown in the field and become a tree,
offering shelter to the birds of the air,
lovingly caressing the nests they prepare.[8]

Your kingdom, like a discovered treasure
hidden for long in a field,
bringing such joy to the finder
that all else rates as nothing.[9]

~

As disciples entrusted with the mysteries of heaven,[10]
we long for the invitation of Jesus –
Come and inherit the kingdom of God,
prepared when the world was founded.[11]

REFERENCES

1) 1 Tim. 6:13–16
2) Luke 1:32, 33
3) Luke 23:42
4) John 18:36, 37
5) Eph. 5:5
6) Matt. 13:43
7) Mark 9:1
8) Matt. 13:31, 32
9) Matt. 13:44–46
10) Matt. 13:11
11) Matt. 25:34

10. *Christ – Liberator*

God, you alone we worship; you alone we serve.
From thirst for status and greed for possessions free us.[1]

~

From violence of all kinds free us, God,
that we may live the gentleness of Jesus.[2]

~

May our hearts be filled with the spirit of the law
that regard for the person be our first concern.[3]

~

When rejected because of our message,
free us from dependence on people.[4]

~

In bodily needs may we know self-control
remembering your Word is nourishment and life.[5]

~

Let human respect never deter us
from reaching out to those in need.[6]

~

God, your giftedness abounds in all your creation.
May sexism not mar this giving.[7]

~

Draw all your people into oneness with you
that all may be brother and sister and mother.[8]

~

May total acceptance be ours at death
and hope become resurrection to glory.[9]

REFERENCES
1) Luke 4:5–8   2) Matt. 26:51, 52, 67
3) Mark 2:23–28   4) John 6:66, 67
5) Matt. 4:1–4   6) Luke 19:5–10
7) John 4:27   8) Matt. 12:46–50
9) John 10:18

11.   *Christ – Messiah*

Christ, the Messiah, has come –
He, the light of all people,
the light that shone in the darkness
that the darkness did not overcome.[1]

~

We pray that everyone may believe in his name
and be given the power to become children of God.[2]

~

Let us know in depth, God, all that Christ proclaims.
Let us hear his voice: 'I am He.'[3]

~

Remembering that he is your Word become flesh,
living among us, showing your glory,
full of grace and truth.[4]

~

Deepen, God, our search for the truth
that we may listen to your voice in Christ.[5]

~

He, sought not glory for himself,
it was you who glorified him.[6]

~

May we too glorify you by our works
and show that you have sent us.[7]

~

Jesus, we will make your name known
to those you give us.[8]

~

Keep us faithful to your word
That we may never see death.[9]

~

We have heard that word.
We believe in the One who sent you.
Thank you for bringing us from death to life –
the gift of life eternal.[10]

REFERENCES
1) John 1:4–13
2) John 1:12
3) John 4:25, 26
4) John 5:24
5) John 18:37
6) John 8:50; 16:14
7) John 8:51
8) John 17:6
9) John 5:36–38
10) John 1:14

12. *Christ – The Mystery*

How great the glory of the mystery
which you, God, have chosen to make known –
the mystery which is Christ in us, the hope of glory.[1]
~
Help us to proclaim and teach in all wisdom
that all may come to maturity in Christ.[2]
~
We thank you, God, for the grace you have given
– the news of the boundless riches of Christ.[3]
~
Let everyone see the plan of the mystery
hidden for ages within you.[4]
~
Gift us anew with the wisdom of your spirit who
     searches even the depths of God.[5]
~
Strengthen us according to the gospel of Jesus,
     proclaiming the mystery kept secret for long ages.[6]
~
Without doubt, the mystery of our religion is great.
We are Christ's servants and stewards of your
     mysteries.[7]
~

Open for us a door for the word,
that we may declare the mystery of Christ.[8]

~

Encourage all hearts and unite us in love
that we may have the riches of assured understanding
and the knowledge of your mystery – Christ himself.[9]

~

With all wisdom, insight and according to your good
    pleasure,
we pray that all things be gathered up in Christ
and live for the praise of his glory.[10]

REFERENCES

1) Col. 1:27
2) Col. 1:28
3) Eph. 3:8
4) Eph. 3:9
5) 1 Cor. 2:9–11
6) Rom. 16:25–27
7) 1 Tim. 3:16; 1 Cor. 4:1
8) Col. 4:3–4
9) Col. 2:2, 3
10) Eph. 1:7–12

13.   *Christ – Obedient*

'See, I have come to do your will'
were the words of Christ coming into the world.[1]
~
Through the offering of the body of Christ for all,
we have now been sanctified.[2]
~
Jesus, your food was to do God's will
– the God who sent you to complete his work.[3]
~
You did nothing on your own
but spoke as God had instructed you.[4]
~
Like you, may we never be left alone
as we strive to do what is pleasing to God.[5]
~
Help us to glorify you, God, on earth
by finishing the work you give us to do.[6]
~
Mould our minds into the mind of Christ Jesus
who emptied himself, obedient to death.[7]
~
'Not my will but yours be done'
was Jesus' prayer in pain and suffering.[8]
~

Let us lose nothing of all you have given
but raise us up, God, on the last day.[9]

~

For this is indeed your will for us
– that all who see and believe in Jesus
may have eternal life.[10]

REFERENCES
1) Heb. 10:5–10
3) John 4:34
5) John 8:29
7) Phil. 2:5–9
9) John 6:38–40

2) Heb. 10:10
4) John 8:28
6) John 17:4
8) Luke 22:42
10) John 6:38–40

14.   *Christ – Praying*

God, your Son Jesus, knowing it was time to choose his
    apostles,
spent time in prayer out in the mountains
– even whole nights in prayer.[1]
~

But as the word about him spread
and people gathered to hear him,
even though crowds clamoured for healing,
he withdrew alone to pray.[2]
~

Jesus, we ask that you teach us to pray
just as you taught your disciples.
'Abba, Father' is our prayer,
our prayer in faith – expectant.[3]
~

We pray for the unity for which Christ prayed
that we may all be one,
remembering our need to pray always with hope.
Fainthearted? Never![4]
~

May your own spirit descend upon us[5]
as we pray in union with Jesus,
praying that trials may never overpower us,
that you keep us always in faith.[6]
~

Let our posture of heart be like that of Jesus:
Father, remove this cup;
yet not my will but yours be done,
whether in times of joy or suffering.[7]

~

You will protect us in your name, our God
– such was the prayer of Jesus –
growing more and more into him
until we are as one.[8]

REFERENCES
1) Luke 6:12
2) Luke 5:15, 16
3) Luke 11:1–4
4) John 17:11; Luke 11:5–8
5) Luke 3:21, 22
6) Luke 22:31, 32
7) Luke 22:41, 42
8) John 17:15, 21–23

15. *Christ – Pre-existing*

In the beginning, God was the Word
and the Word was with you
and the Word was you.[1]

~

Through the Word all things came into being.
Without the Word, nothing had life.[2]
In truth, Jesus could openly proclaim:
'Before Abraham was, I am.'[3]

~

You have made your Son, Jesus, heir of all things
– Jesus, the reflection of your own glory;
the imprint of your very being.[4]

~

All things are sustained by your powerful Word
– the Word now seated at your right hand,
the right hand of your majesty on high.[5]

~

Jesus, you proclaimed what you had seen and heard
– you, the one who comes from heaven.[6]

~

In you, God has chosen us to be holy and blameless;
chosen before the foundation of the world.[7]

~

You are the image of the invisible God,
the first born of all creation.
In you were created all things in heaven and on earth.[8]

~

You yourself are before all things
and in you all things hold together.
The fullness of God was pleased to dwell in you.[9]

~

Though you were in the form of God,
you did not exploit the equality.
You emptied yourself and became as a slave,
obedient to death on a cross.[10]

~

So, let every creature in heaven and on earth,
and all that is in the sea,
give blessing, honour, glory and might
to the Lamb who was slain, forever.[11]

REFERENCES
1) John 1:1
2) John 1:2, 3
3) John 8:58
4) Heb. 1:1–3
5) Heb. 1:3, 4
6) John 3:31, 32
7) Eph. 1:4
8) Col. 1:15, 16
9) Col. 1:17–19
10) Phil. 2:6–8
11) Rev. 5:11–14

16.   *Christ – Shepherd*

In the past, God, you called yourself 'Shepherd of Israel'
and your Son Jesus is our good shepherd.[1]
~

As the sheep know the voice of their shepherd
may we know your voice in the midst of life's turmoil.[2]
~

Like Jesus, may we be among your own,
encountering you ever more deeply.[3]
~

Look on your people harassed and helpless,
like sheep without a shepherd.[4]
~

Help us extend a welcome to all
– 'one flock, one shepherd', Christ's prayer.[5]
~

Increase the Jesus life in us,
life in abundance, life to the full.[6]
~

In our shepherding may we be prepared
to lay down our lives for others.[7]
~

Bring us to own our need to change
as the shepherds knew their need.
They were the first to hear the good news
– the news of Jesus' birth.[8]

May we be examples to all the flock,
journeying in faith together,
and you, the chief shepherd, will give us the crown
– the crown of unfading glory.[9]

REFERENCES
1) John 10:11
2) John 10:4
3) John 10:14, 15
4) Matt. 9:36
5) John 10:16
6) John 10:10
7) John 10:17
8) Luke 2:8–20
9) 1 Pet. 5:3, 4

17. Christ – Suffering

'My Father, if it is possible,
let this cup pass from me.
Yet, not what I want but what you want.'[1]

~

For this is the blood of the covenant,
poured out for many, for the forgiveness of sins.[2]

~

We pray, God, for courage in our own times of passion.
Our spirit is indeed willing but our flesh is weak.[3]

~

Give us the wisdom to know when to speak
and the Christ-likeness that enables silence.[4]

~

In desolate moments, let us join in your prayer:
'My God, my God, why have you forsaken me?'[5]

~

Move deeply our hearts, God, as we ponder Christ's
    passion,
like the whole of creation that quaked in shock.[6]

~

Let us never, like Pilate, wash away our guilt,
as Jesus is again slain in the atrocities of war.[7]

~

Like the women on Calvary, true to the end,
may nothing weaken our discipleship.[8]

Remembering the promise of Christ's resurrection:
He will be raised immortal.[9]

REFERENCES
1) Matt. 26:39
2) Matt. 26:28
3) Matt. 26:41
4) Matt. 27:14
5) Matt. 27:46
6) Matt. 27:51–53
7) Matt. 27:24
8) Matt. 27:56
9) Matt. 20:19

18. *Compassion*

God, as your chosen ones, holy and beloved,
clothe us with compassion and kindness.[1]

~

Like Jesus, may we be moved with compassion
as we reach out to others with healing.[2]

~

God, you are compassionate and merciful.
Make us your mercy, your compassion.[3]

~

Let us be shepherds, one to another,
ready to teach with compassion.[4]

~

By your loving mercy, your tender compassion,
the dawn from on high has broken upon us.[5]

~

'Do not weep' were Jesus' own words of compassion
to the widow, bereft and grieving.[6]

~

And the leprous body drew forth deep compassion:
'I do choose,' said Jesus and healed him.[7]

~

We long to experience the compassion of Christ.
God, fulfil our longing.[8]

~

Give us hearts that are gentle and humble,
merging evermore into Jesus.[9]

~

With sympathy, love and unity of spirit,
may tenderness dwell in our hearts.[10]

REFERENCES
1) Col. 3:12   2) Mark 1:41
3) Jas 5:11   4) Mark 6:34
5) Luke 1:76–78   6) Luke 7:13
7) Mark 1:41   8) Phil. 1:8
9) Matt. 11:29   10) 1 Pet. 3:8

19.   *Conscience*

With a clear conscience,
let us hold to the mystery of faith,
thanking God as our ancestors did.[1]

~

In everything, let us aim for a clear conscience,
clear before God and all,
for God sees us as we are.
May our conscience do so too.[2]

~

When asked the reason for our hope,
let us have our answer ready;
given with courtesy, conscience clear,
showing respect for all.[3]

~

Faith, God and a good conscience are our weapons.
May our faith not be wrecked by ignoring our
    conscience.[4]

~

True, our conscience may not reproach us
but that does not mean justification.
God is our judge.[5]

~

Let us then be obedient,
not only because of retribution,
but also for conscience's sake.[6]

In truth not pretence,
let us speak in Christ,
our conscience testifying for us
in the Holy Spirit.[7]

REFERENCES
1) 1 Tim. 3:9; 2 Tim. 1:3
3) 1 Pet. 3:15
5) 1 Cor. 4:4
7) Rom. 9:1

2) Acts 24:16; 2 Cor. 5:11
4) 1 Tim. 1:19
6) Rom. 13:5

20. *Covenant*

God, you are blessed forever and ever.
You chose a people to be your own.[1]

~

To them the covenant and the promises belong
and from their patriarchs according to the flesh,
the Messiah, Jesus, came.[2]

~

In Jesus, we who once were far off
have been brought near by the blood of Christ.[3]

~

The promises were made to Abraham and his offspring,
that is, to one person who is Christ.[4]

~

We thank you, Jesus, for the covenant of your blood,
poured out for us and for many.[5]

~

We pray that, like you, we may become 'yes'
– 'yes' to every one of God's promises.[6]

~

Through you, the mediator of the new covenant,
we can receive the promised inheritance.[7]

~

Deepen in us, God, the Spirit of covenant,
giving life to our ministry with others.[8]

~

We thank you for looking on us with favour
and redeeming us through Jesus, a mighty saviour.[9]

~

Remember your covenant with us always,
that we may serve you in holiness, all our days.[10]

REFERENCES
1) Eph. 1:3, 4
3) Eph. 2:13
5) Mark 14:24
7) Heb. 9:15
9) Luke 1:68, 69

2) Rom. 9:4, 5
4) Gal. 3:16
6) 2 Cor. 1:19, 20
8) 2 Cor. 3:4–6
10) Luke 1:70–74

21. *Co-workers with God*

God, you are rich in mercy and loved us even as sinners.
You made us alive, together with Christ.
Your grace has saved us.[1]

~

Help us declare what we have seen and heard,
then fellowship is ours and joy complete.[2]

~

We pray that our sharing of faith be effective,
as we see all the good we can do for Christ.[3]

~

Our goal is to be with you, God, forever.
With these words let us encourage one another.[4]

~

We share in the grace of God together.
Let us hold one another in our hearts.[5]

~

In our giving and receiving may we all be free
– always in the spirit of the Gospel.[6]

~

Devoting ourselves to the message of Jesus,
and growing more truly in fellowship.[7]

~

We want to know Christ and the power of his rising,
sharing his sufferings – like him in his death.[8]

~

If we are God's children, we are also his heirs,
heirs of God together and joint heirs with Christ.[9]

~

Let us be partners and co-workers in service,
sharing God's grace in fellowship.[10]

REFERENCES
1) Eph. 2:4, 5
2) 1 John 1:3, 4
3) Philem. v. 6
4) 1 Thess. 4:17, 18
5) Phil. 1:7
6) Phil. 4:15
7) Acts 2:42
8) Phil. 3:10
9) Rom. 8:17
10) 2 Cor. 8:23

22.   *Death*

God, your Son Jesus came, not to be served
but to give his life, a ransom for many.[1]
~

Give me grace to give over to death
whatever in me is greed and evil.[2]
~

Though willing to remain and share the Good News,
deepen my desire to be with Christ.[3]
~

Whether by life or by death, may Christ be exalted,
now and always, in my body.[4]
~

Sin entered the world and through sin came death
and death spread to everyone,
because all have sinned.[5]
But we are justified by your grace,
gifted to us through redemption in Jesus.[6]
~

So we glorify you, God, in our bodies,
for we were bought at an ultimate price.[7]
This is my blood, poured out for many
that sins might be forgiven.[8]
~

Having fought the good fight and finished the race,
may we, like Jesus, at the moment of death,
yield our spirit into your hands.[9]

~

Who will save me from this body of death?
Thanks to you, God,
for the victory through Christ.[10]

REFERENCES

1) Matt. 20:28
2) Col. 3:5
3) Phil. 1:23–26
4) Phil. 1:20
5) Rom. 5:12
6) Rom. 3:24
7) 1 Cor. 6:20
8) Matt. 26:28
9) 2 Tim. 4:6–8; Matt. 27:50
10) Rom. 7:24

23. *Detachment*

As the wheat grain falls into the ground and dies,
it bears abundant fruit.
May we die to selfish life in this world,
remembering life eternal.[1]

~

Make us strong, God, with the strength of your power
against the spiritual forces of evil.[2]

~

In discipline, alertness and self control
let us resist, steadfast in faith.[3]

~

Our old corrupt self has been put away.
In your likeness, God, renew us.[4]

~

Gift us with contentment of heart, God
– contentment with what we have.[5]

~

Like the poor widow who gave her very last coin,
mould us into total giving.[6]

~

Though life be fading, may we never lose heart.
Our inner nature is renewed day by day.[7]

~

All is your gift, God, let us hold things in common,
sharing with all those in need.[8]

Detach us from the love of possessions and wealth.
Let us follow your Son without grieving.[9]

~

Bring us to see everything as loss, for Christ,
that we may be found in him.[10]

REFERENCES
1) John 12:24–26
2) Eph. 6:10–17
3) 1 Cor. 9:25; 1 Pet. 5:9
4) Eph. 4:22–24
5) 1 Tim. 6:6–10
6) Luke 21:1–4
7) 2 Cor. 4:16–18
8) Acts 2:44, 45
9) Matt. 19:16–22
10) Phil. 3:7–9

24. *Discernment*

God, we are from you.
We believe your words.
Give us open minds and hearts
to hear and discern more deeply.[1]

∿

Though we have never heard your voice
nor seen your form
let your word abide in us.
We believe in the One you sent.[2]

∿

So keep all foolishness from our lives
and lead us in understanding your will.[3]

∿

Fill us with the knowledge of your will
in all spiritual wisdom and understanding.
Then our lives can be worthy of you,
bearing fruit in every good work.[4]

∿

Transform us, God, by renewing our minds
that we may discern your will,
trying to discover what is pleasing to you,
what is good, acceptable and perfect.[5*6]

∿

Release in us the gifts of your Spirit
that we may discern all things.
Praying for one another
we come to maturity and assurance in all that you will.[7&8]

~

May you, the God of peace,
who brought back Jesus from the dead,
make us complete in everything good
– all that is pleasing in your sight.[9]

REFERENCES
1) John 8:47
2) John 5:37, 38
3) Eph. 5:17
4) Col. 1:9, 10
5) Eph. 5:10
6) Rom. 12:2
7) 1 Cor. 2:14, 15
8) Col. 4:12
9) Heb. 13:20, 21

25.   *Discipleship*

Divest us, God, of unnecessary possessions
that we may be true disciples.[1]
~
Teach us to pray 'Abba, Father'
as Jesus taught his disciples.[2]
~
You send us to proclaim your kingdom
and empower us with your healing.[3]
~
Detach us from family – yes, life itself –
freedom for total discipleship.[4]
~
Let us be servants one to another
remembering the example of Jesus.[5]
~
Living his new commandment of love,
the true mark of Jesus' disciple.[6]
~
Make us continue in the word of Jesus.
Then we are disciples indeed.[7]
~
Open our hearts to learn from your Son
– the humble, gentle Jesus.
His yoke is easy and his burden light.
We will find rest for our souls.[8]

May we cling to the way we have learned from Christ,
avoiding all that is evil.[9]

~

Remembering Jesus is with us always,
yes, to the end of the world.[10]

REFERENCES

1) Luke 14:33
2) Luke 11:1
3) Luke 9:1, 2
4) Luke 14:26, 27
5) John 13:12–15
6) John 13:34, 35
7) John 8:31, 32
8) Matt. 11:28–30
9) 2 Tim. 3:13–15
10) Matt. 28:20

26. *Ecology*

God, like Jesus your Son – son of the soil,
merge us into oneness with nature.

~

Like the lilies of the field and the birds of the air,
lift us from undue anxiety.[1]

~

Make us more truly the salt of the earth,
cherishing each part of creation.[2]

~

And temper our greed when digging the earth;
remind us that all is sacred.[3]

~

Build up our faith in times of terror;
let us hear your 'Peace, be still.'[4]

~

And help us respect even the ground we tread;
in agony, a rock of support.[5]

~

May we be a leaven in the midst of our world
diffusing appreciation and reverence.[6]

~

And may contentment be ours in little things
– a manger, a mustard seed, a loaf.[7, 8 & 9]

~

Make our hearts grateful for the sun and the rains
given to all out of love.[10]

~

And help us keep pure the environment we enjoy;
we punish ourselves in destroying.[11]

~

As the sun's light failed at the death of Jesus,
may the earth too mourn our passing.[12]

~

Let us wait for your promise –
a new earth, a new heaven
and righteousness at home with all.[13]

REFERENCES

1) Matt. 6:28–30
2) Matt. 5:13
3) Matt. 13:44
4) Mark 4:39, 40
5) Matt. 26:39
6) Matt. 13:33
7) Luke 2:7
8) Mark 4:30–32
9) Matt. 13:33
10) Matt. 5:44, 45
11) John 21:3
12) Luke 23:44, 45
13) 2 Pet. 3:13

27. *Encouragement*

With encouragement, let us share the truth with one
    another;
dispersing falsehood and error with careful instruction.[1]
~

Much joy and encouragement stem from love
setting at rest the hearts of God's holy people.[2]
~

Today and every day, encourage one another,
avoiding the lure of sin and its hardening[3]
for we have been given a share in Christ
if we hold our first confidence to the end.[4]
~

The gift of prophecy speaks to others,
building, encouraging and giving reassurance.[5]
~

Through encouragement, fresh heart is experienced
and perseverance in faith strengthened.[6]
~

In all ways encouragement can be offered
through the written word and the shared experience,[7]
bringing delight to the hearts of all.[8]
~

In hardship, doubt and times of distress
encouraging words can lift the spirit,
affirmation and hospitality giving strength for
    the journey.[9]

REFERENCES
1) 2 Tim. 4:2   2) Philem. v. 7
3) Heb. 3:13   4) Heb. 3:14
5) 1 Cor. 14:3   6) Acts 14:22
7) Acts 15:30, 31   8) Acts 15:31
9) Acts 16:40; 18:27

28. *Endurance*

Remembering not a hair of our head will perish,
give us grace, God, to endure.[1]

~

Direct our hearts to your own love
and lead us to the steadfastness of Christ.[2]

~

Deepen our spirit of prayerfulness
that we may never lose heart[3]
but endure like the saints who kept your law
and held fast to the faith of Jesus.[4]

~

Indeed we are blessed in showing endurance.
The crown of life will be ours.[5]

~

Even endurance in suffering for right
is our call as disciples of Jesus.
He has left an example
for us to follow in his steps.[6]

~

Enduring all for the sake of the elect
that they may obtain salvation.
If we have endured with Jesus,
with him we shall also reign.[7]

~

God of steadfastness,
grant us to live in harmony with one another[8]
pursuing righteousness, godliness and faith,
gentleness, love and endurance.[9]

~

When hated because of your name, God,
strengthen us to endure to the end.[10]

~

Let the people be aware of our steadfastness.
In affliction – our faith, our endurance.[11]

REFERENCES
1) Luke 21:18, 19
2) 2 Thess. 3:5
3) Luke 18:1
4) Rev. 14:12
5) Jas 5:11; 1:12
6) 1 Pet. 2:20, 21
7) 2 Tim. 2:10–12
8) Rom. 15:5, 6
9) 1 Tim. 6:11
10) Mark 13:13
11) 2 Thess. 1:4

29. *Eucharist*

We thank you, God, for giving us through Jesus,
the food that endures for eternal life.[1]

~

Strengthen our faith
that we may believe ever more deeply
in the one you have sent.[2]

~

Jesus, bread of life, we hunger for you.
Quench our thirst as we open in faith.[3]

~

Our ancestors ate manna in the wilderness and died
but we who eat of the bread from heaven
we will not die.[4]

~

Jesus, you are the living bread.
You give your flesh for the life of the world.
Let us eat this bread and live forever
– the bread of life, freely given.[5]

~

Your own words tell us, Jesus,
that unless we eat your flesh
and drink your blood,
we have no life in us.[6]

~

But if we eat and if we drink, we have eternal life
and on the last day, we will know resurrection
for you will raise us up.[7]

~

Your flesh is true food and your blood is true drink.
Abide in us, Jesus.
May we abide in you.[8]

~

In coming to you we will never be hungry.
By believing in you we will never thirst.
You will not drive away anyone who comes.[9]
Of all God has given you, you will lose nothing.[10]

REFERENCES
1) John 6:27
2) John 6:29
3) John 6:35
4) John 6:49, 50
5) John 6:51
6) John 6:53
7) John 6:54
8) John 6:56
9) John 6:37
10) John 6:39

30. *Faith*

God, you are faithful – faithful forever.
You cannot deny yourself.[1]
~
Give us the assurance of things we hope for
and the conviction of things unseen.[2]
~
In total trust, like that of Abraham,
may we step out in faith – unknowing.[3]
~
Deepen our faith in Jesus your Son
and eternal life is ours.[4]
~
May your word abide in us forever,
believing in the One whom you sent.[5]
~
For, as Jesus died and rose again
our death becomes resurrection through Jesus.[6]
~
Like the grass of the field clothed by your hand,
may we of little faith know surrender.[7]
~
Nourish our belief in scripture – in the word,
the word that Jesus has spoken.[8]
~

Remembering that suffering accompanies faith,
a privilege graciously granted.[9]

~

God, help us be faithful even till death.
You will give us the crown of life.[10]

REFERENCES
1) 2 Tim. 2:13
2) Heb. 11:1–3
3) Heb. 11:8
4) John 3:34–36
5) John 5:37, 38
6) 1 Thess. 4:14
7) Matt. 6:30, 31
8) John 2:22
9) Phil. 1:29
10) Rev. 2:10

31. *The Family*

God, gift all parents with deep and lively faith
like the faith of our ancestors,
handed on through generations.[1]

~

May the love of husbands for their own bodies
be the same love with which they cherish their wives.[2]

~

May wives love their husbands
and tenderly relish their children,
making for all a home of warmth and orderliness.[3]

~

Strengthen young men, God, in self control,
enabling moderation in everything.[4]

~

As fathers may they instruct, not provoke their children,
so that during life's journey they never lose heart.[5]

~

Keep young women, God, self-controlled and chaste,
valuing the right behaviour of women before them.[6]

~

Gift all mothers with kindness in plenty
and bless the children within our families
with a spirit of obedience and trust.[7]

~

Let all provide for relatives and family members,
for this is our duty in faith.[8]

~

A 'great mystery' – marriage!
Two become one, imaging Christ and his Church.[9]

REFERENCES
1) 2 Tim. 1:3–5
3) Titus 2:4, 5
5) Col. 3:21
7) Col. 3:20
9) Eph. 5:31, 32
2) Eph. 5:25–33
4) Titus 2:6
6) Titus 2:3–6
8) 1 Tim. 5:8

Note: The biblical Greek word 'musterion' (mystery) means
something so beautifully deep that it is endlessly rich.

32. *Fatherhood*

God, one and only, our Father,
all things are from you.
For you we exist.[1]

~

We bow our knee before you,
from whom, in heaven and on earth,
every family takes its name.[2]

~

Help all fathers to gift their children
with what is right and good.[3]

~

And give them the wisdom
to lead their sons in working together as one.[4]

~

In times that call for celebration,
let there be joy in abundance.[5]

~

And when forgiveness is required,
may fathers be generous in giving.[6]

~

Realizing also the need for discipline
and guidance in your ways.[7]

~

Making a home, like Joseph of old,
with skill and fatherly care.[8]

A father, pleading a cure for his child,[9]
an instructor, God, in your ways,[10]
never provoking; they may lose heart
– a person of patience and faith.[11]

~

One body, one spirit, one hope in our calling,
one Lord, one faith, and one baptism.
One God and Father of all, above all,
through all and in all forever.[12]

REFERENCES
1) 1 Cor. 8:6
3) Luke 11:11–13
5) Matt. 22:1, 2
7) Heb. 12:7
9) Luke 8:40–42
11) Col. 3:21

2) Eph. 3:14, 15
4) Matt. 21:28–31
6) Luke 15:11–13
8) Matt. 2:19–23
10) Eph. 6:4
12) Eph. 4:4–6

33. *Fellowship*

Your divine power, God, has given us all we need,
and the promises through which we participate in your
   divine nature.[1]

~

You are a faithful God, calling us into fellowship
– fellowship with Jesus, your Son.[2]

~

Let us try to find what is pleasing to you,
having no part in unfruitful works of darkness.[3]

~

We were buried with Christ in baptism
and raised with him through faith
– faith in your power, O God.[4]

~

Make us walk as children of the light.
What fellowship is there between light and darkness?[5]

~

The cup we bless – a sharing in Christ's blood.
The bread we break – a sharing in his body.
One bread, one body;
though many, we are one.[6]

~

In struggle and love we die together.
In struggle and love we live together.
We carry each one in our hearts.[7]

Help us become all things to all people
for the sake of the gospel
and to share in its blessings.[8]

~

If we die with Christ we will live with him,
so let us be dead to sin
and alive to you in Christ Jesus.[9]

~

The grace of our Lord Jesus Christ,
the love of God
and the fellowship of the Holy Spirit
be with us all.[10]

REFERENCES
1) 2 Pet. 1:3, 4   2) 1 Cor. 1:9
3) Eph. 5:11   4) Rom. 6:4, 5
5) 2 Cor. 6:14   6) 2 Cor. 6:11–13
7) 2 Cor. 7:3   8) 1 Cor. 9:22, 23
9) Rom. 6:8–11   10) 2 Cor. 13:13

34. *Forgiveness*

Blessed are you, God the Father of our Lord Jesus Christ,
the God of mercies and of all consolation.[1]

~

In Jesus, we have redemption through his blood
and forgiveness of our sins
through the riches of his grace, lavished upon us.[2]

~

In truth, we can pray:
where sin increased, grace did all the more abound.[3]

~

Let us then put away all bitterness and wrath,
all anger, wrangling and slander, malice of every kind.[4]

~

Touch our hearts, God, that we may be kind to one
     another,
tender hearted, ready to forgive
as you in Christ have forgiven us.[5]

~

May we never repay evil for evil
but sincerely seek to do good,
good to one another and to all.[6]

~

Let our prayer, in union with Jesus, ever be:
'Father, forgive them;
they do not know what they are doing.'[7]

As your sun, God, shines on the good and the evil
and your rain falls freely on all,
mould us into total loving –
our prayer embracing everyone.[8]

REFERENCES
1) 2 Cor. 1:3
2) Eph. 1:7, 8
3) Rom. 5:20
4) Eph. 4:31
5) Eph. 4:32–5:2
6) 1 Thess. 5:15
7) Luke 23:34
8) Matt. 5:44–45

35.   *Freedom*

'Where the spirit of the Lord is, there is freedom.'
Free us, God, in your spirit.[1]
~
For we know we are called to freedom
in loving service to one another.[2]
~
For freedom, Christ has set us free.
Let us stand firm against unfreedom.[3]
~
May this liberty not be a stumbling block to others,[4]
never using freedom as a pretext for evil.[5]
~
Bring us more deeply into discipleship.
May we continue in the word of Jesus.
Then we will know the truth
and the truth will make us free.[6]
~
We are justified, God, by the free gift of your grace,
through being set free in Christ Jesus.[7]
~
May creation be freed from its slavery to corruption,
to enjoy this same glorious freedom.[8]

REFERENCES

1) 2 Cor. 3:17   2) Gal. 5:13
3) Gal. 5:1   4) 1 Cor. 8:8, 9
5) 1 Pet. 2:16   6) John 8:31–36
7) Rom. 3:24   8) Rom. 8:21

36.   *Friendship*

Thank you, God, for the gift of friendship.
The peacemakers, the friend makers are blessed.[1]

~

Lead us to celebrate together with friends
in mutual love rejoicing.[2]

~

Greeting each one in person by name,
sharing friendship and peace.[3]

~

In company, giving and receiving refreshment,
listening and praying as one.[4]

~

When forgiveness is needed, help us, God,
that our friendship may deepen and grow.[5]

~

Knowing even friends can hurt one another,
make us sincere and open.[6]

~

Sharing your goodness, God, working within,
knowing your presence, your love.[7]

~

With the comforting power of your Spirit, God,
may we too comfort each other.[8]

~

In friendship, make genuine our concern for the other.
Bring us to caring in depth.[9]

~

With gratitude for the gift of 'friend',
let us pray, day and night, in our hearts.[10]

REFERENCES
1) Matt. 5:9
2) Luke 15:6
3) Rom. 16:1–23
4) Rom. 15:30, 32
5) Matt. 26:50
6) 2 Cor. 6:11–13
7) Mark 5:18–20; Rom. 5:5
8) Col. 4:10, 11
9) Phil. 2:20
10) 2 Tim. 1:3

37.   *Fruit*

Nurture in us, God, the fruit of your Spirit
– love, joy, patience and peace.
Make our hearts gentle, generous
and kind in self control and faithfulness.[1]

~

Give us the wisdom, pure and from above,
gentle, peaceable, willingness to yield.
Then mercy and good works will flow.[2]

~

We have been given your kingdom, God.
May its fruits show forth in our lives.[3]
In ministry, sharing and receiving fruit
when coming together as one.[4]

~

Let us show the peaceful fruit of righteousness
that comes from discipline and pain.[5]

~

The fruit we bear is the fruit of repentance.
By our fruits let us be known.[6]

~

We have died to the law through the body of Christ
and now we belong to another,
to Christ, risen from death to life
that we might bear fruit for God.[7]

~

When blessed with gifts that are temporal
may we seek the spiritual fruits.[8]
Remembering too the false prophets of today;
we will know them by their fruits.[9]

~

Living in Christ means fruitful labour.
Dying in Christ is gain.
Give us grace, God, to accept life or death
– whatever – in his name.[10]

REFERENCES
1) Gal. 5:22, 23   2) Jas 3:17
3) Matt. 21:43   4) Rom. 1:11–13
5) Heb. 12:11   6) Matt. 3:7, 8
7) Rom. 7:4   8) Phil. 4:16, 17
9) Matt. 7:15–20   10) Phil. 1:21–24

38. *Glory*

Let us join with the multitude of the heavenly host
    saying:
'Glory to God in the highest.'[1]

~

To you, God, belong the glory and the power.
Yes, forever and ever.[2]

~

There is no need of sun or moon
in the city of the new Jerusalem,
for your glory, God, is its light.
Its lamp is indeed the Lamb.[3]

~

Jesus is the reflection of your own glory,
the exact imprint of your very being.[4]

~

We were buried with him by baptism into death
and raised from the dead by the glory that is yours.[5]

~

Though we have sinned and fallen short of your glory,
we are justified by your gift of grace
through redemption in Christ Jesus.[6]

~

Like the disciples on Tabor, let us see your glory.
When Christ who is our life, is revealed,
we too will be revealed in glory.[7]

Bring us to imperishability, God.
Raise us in glory.[8]

~

We ask you to glorify your name in us.
Let us hear your words:
'I have glorified it and will glorify it again.'[9]

~

God of peace, make us complete in everything good,
all that is pleasing in your sight,
through Jesus Christ, to whom be the glory
forever and ever, Amen.[10]

REFERENCES
1) Luke 2:13, 14
2) 1 Pet. 4:11
3) Rev. 21:22–26
4) Heb. 1:3
5) Rom. 6:4, 5
6) Rom. 3:23, 24
7) Luke 9:28–36; 1 John 3:2
8) 1 Cor. 15:42, 43
9) John 12:28
10) Heb. 13:20, 21

39. *God's Love*

God, you loved the world so much,
you gave your only Son.
Bring all to faith in Jesus,
that eternal life may be theirs.[1]

~

We want to remain in the love of Jesus.
It was for us that Jesus prayed.[2]

~

Let us be shepherd one to another,
ready to lay down our lives.[3]

~

For no one has greater love than this:
to lay down one's life for one's friends.[4]

~

Your own love, God, has been poured into our hearts
by the Holy Spirit, which has been given to us.[5]

~

Jesus, you gave proof of God's love for us.
While we were still sinners, you died for us.[6]

~

The fruit of the spirit is love.
Mould us into purest love.[7]

~

We know that whoever fails to love
does not know the God of love.
You are love itself.
Steep us in your love.[8]

~

God, you are rich in faithful love
and through your love you raised us in Christ
and gave us a place with him in heaven.[9]

~

Bring us to know deeply your love
– the love beyond all knowledge.
Fill us with the utter fullness that is yours.[10]

REFERENCES

1) John 3:16
2) John 15:9; 17:9
3) John 10:11
4) John 15:12, 13
5) Rom. 5:5
6) Rom. 5:7, 8
7) Gal. 5:22
8) 1 John 4:8–10
9) Eph. 2:4–6
10) Eph. 3:19

40. *God in All*

God, we know that no idol exists,
that there is no God but you.
You, the one from whom are all things,
for whom we all exist.[1]

~

O the depths of the riches
of your wisdom and knowledge.
Unsearchable your judgements;
inscrutable your ways.[2]

~

We cannot know your mind, our God.
We can never be your counsellor.
Impossible for us to give you a gift
and receive a gift in return.[3]

~

For from you, through you and to you are all things.
To you be glory, forever.[4]

~

You are the blessed and only Sovereign,
the King of kings and Lord of lords.[5]

~

Alone immortal, dwelling in light unapproachable.
No one has seen you.
No one can see you.
To you be honour and eternal dominion.[6]

Everything needed for life, you have given,
everything pertaining to godliness.[7]

~

Keep us, God, from the corruption in our world,
and so remain participants in your divine nature.[8]

~

You who made the world and everything in it
– not contained in shrines human made,
never far from each one of us –
in you we live, move, and have our being.[9]

~

Let us own your presence in all of creation
– in everything you have made.
To you, our God, whom we know and honour,
we give praise and thanks unceasingly.[10]

REFERENCES
1) 1 Cor. 8:4–6
2) Rom. 11:33
3) Rom. 11:34, 35
4) Rom. 11:36
5) 1 Tim. 6:15
6) 1 Tim. 6:16
7) 2 Pet. 1:3
8) 2 Pet. 1:4
9) Acts 17:24–28
10) Rom. 1:18–21

41. *Gratitude*

Giving thanks, we receive the bread
blessed – broken – shared.
We take and eat the body of the Lord
given up for us and for all.[1]

~

We take the cup while giving thanks,
the cup shed for us and for many.
The blood of Jesus, we take and drink.
We do so in memory of him.[2]

~

Having received Jesus as Lord and Christ
we live our lives in him
rooted, built up, held firm by faith.
Our hearts with thanksgiving overflow.[3]

~

Unworried our lives as we gratefully share with God
our desires, our needs.
And a peace unspeakable, the peace of God
guards our thoughts in Christ.[4]

~

God, all your creation is good;
no food to be rejected.
Made holy by your word and prayer,
may all be received with thanksgiving.[5]

We thank you too, for the faith of one another
– our encouragement in times of distress.[6]

~

In Jesus, we have been given your grace,
drawing forth constant thanksgiving.
And richly endowed in all utterance and knowledge
we thank you, God.[7]

~

Let us then sing psalms and hymns and inspired songs,
singing and chanting to God in our hearts,
giving thanks to the Father through Jesus.[8]

~

In Christ, you lead us in triumph,
as through us the fragrance of knowing you is spread.
We thank you, God.[9]

REFERENCES
1) Luke 22:19
2) Matt. 26:27, 28
3) Col. 2:6, 7
4) Phil. 4:6, 7
5) 1 Tim.4: 4, 5
6) 1 Thess. 3:7–9
7) 1 Cor. 1:4, 5
8) Eph. 5:19, 20
9) 2 Cor. 2:14

42. *Healing*

God, heal the dullness of our hearts,
that we may listen and hear,
look and indeed perceive.[1]

~

Use your power and restore our world.
Let all people know your healing touch.[2]

~

May the least and the greatest experience your healing.
Bless us always with someone to care.[3]

~

Send us anew to proclaim your kingdom
– with authority and power to heal.[4]

~

Even when the moment of death draws near,
your healing touch can save.[5]

~

Open our eyes and soften our hearts,
that understanding and healing will be ours.[6]

~

Take away, God, our hardness of hearing,
our blindness that cannot see.
Gift us with listening, understanding hearts.
Let us turn to you and be healed.[7]

REFERENCES

1) Matt. 13:15
2) Luke 5:17
3) Luke 7:2, 3
4) Luke 9:2
5) John 4:46, 47
6) John 12:40
7) Matt. 13:15

43. *Heart*

God, you know everyone's heart,
our feelings, passions, desires.[1]
~
You are the searcher of mind and heart.
Release your Spirit within us.[2]
~
Let not hardness seep into our hearts.
Your kindness can lead to repentance.[3]
~
Keep us faithful with steadfast devotion,
full of the Holy Spirit and faith.[4]
~
Knowing your love is poured into our hearts
by your own free gift of the Spirit.[5]
~
May Christ dwell in our hearts through faith,
grounding, rooting us in love.[6]
~
On our hearts, God, your covenant is written:
you are our God; we are your people.[7]
~
As the morning star rises in our hearts,
open us to your message.[8]
~

With humble mind and heart that is tender,
bring us to sympathy and love for one another.[9]

~

And as we grow into unity of spirit,
let us refresh each heart in Christ.[10]

REFERENCES

1) Acts 1:24
2) Rom. 8:27
3) Mark 10:5; Rom. 2:4
4) Acts 11:23, 24
5) Rom. 5:5
6) Eph. 3:17
7) Heb. 8:10
8) 2 Pet. 1:19
9) 1 Pet. 3:8
10) Philem. v. 20

44. *Holiness*

'Holy, holy, holy
the Lord God the almighty
who was and is and is to come.'[1]
~
We pray with Jesus,
that your name be held holy.[2]
~
We want to be holy.
You have called us to this.[3]
~
You are the one who sanctifies.[4]
~
We thank you for making us a holy nation
– yes, your very own people.[5]
~
Your grace is able to build us up
and to give us the inheritance
among all who are sanctified.[6]
~
We have been chosen as the first fruits for salvation
and through belief in the truth,
we are sanctified by the Spirit.[7]
~
Strengthen our hearts in holiness, God,
that we may be blameless at the coming of Jesus.[8]

Jesus, in accordance with your will,
offered his body once and for all,
enabling our pathway to holiness.[9]

~

May we present our bodies to you, our God,
as a living sacrifice – acceptable and holy.[10]

~

Remembering that we were washed and sanctified,
justified in the name of Jesus, your Son,
and in the power of your Spirit.[11]

~

Let us greet one another with a holy kiss,
as we journey towards holiness complete.[12]

REFERENCES
1) Rev. 4:8
2) Matt. 6:9
3) 1 Pet. 1:14–16
4) Heb. 2:11
5) 1 Pet. 2:9
6) Acts 20:32
7) 2 Thess. 2:13
8) 1 Thess. 3:13
9) Heb. 10:10
10) Rom. 12:1
11) 1 Cor. 6:11
12) 1 Cor. 16:19, 20

45. *The Holy Spirit*

God, send your Spirit upon us
that we as your anointed ones
may bring good news to the poor.[1]

~

Send us to proclaim release to the captives,
to the blind recovery of sight
and to let the oppressed go free.[1]

~

We want to be your witnesses.
Give us the power of your Spirit.[2]

~

Open our hearts to the guidance of your Spirit
– openness like that of Simeon,[3]
knowing your Spirit will always teach us what we ought
    to say.[4]

~

Build up our togetherness and gift us with peace.
May we know your Spirit's comforting.[5]

~

May the Spirit so fill our minds and hearts
that we speak your word with boldness.[6]

~

Let us know in fullness your Spirit's joy,
even when captive to the Spirit, unknowing.[7]

~

Send your Holy Spirit anew on the earth,
overshadowing it with your power,
that all may be birthed into holiness
and be called children of God.[8]

~

We thank you, God of heaven and earth,
and we rejoice in your Holy Spirit,
for things you have hidden from the wise and intelligent,
you have revealed to infants.[9]

~

Our prayer is that all may receive your Spirit,
that you lay your hands gently on all.[10]

~

Like Stephen, may we be filled with the Spirit
and gaze on your glory in heaven.[11]

REFERENCES
1) Luke 4:18   2) Acts 1:8
3) Luke 2:27   4) Luke 12:12
5) Acts 9:31   6) Acts 4:31
7) Acts 13:51; 20:22   8) Luke 1:35
9) Luke 10:21   10) Acts 8:14, 17
11) Acts 7:55

46. *Hope*

In hope, we were saved.
As we wait in patience for what we do not see,
grace us, God, with hope.[1]

~

Make possible our hoping, even against hope,
like Abraham, the father of many nations.[2]

~

You are the God of hope.
Fill us with hope in abundance
by the power of your Holy Spirit.[3]

~

In hopeful rejoicing,
let us even boast of our hope of sharing your glory.[4]

~

In steadfastness, God, let us hold to your word,
open to the encouragement of the Scriptures in hope.[5]

~

Remembering Christ is among us always.
He is the hope of Glory.[6]

~

Purify us, God, in our hoping,
that we may be pure as you are pure.[7]

~

God of truth, lead us to seize the hope set before us
– a sure and steadfast anchor of the soul.[8]

As a lamp shining in a dark place,
make us attentive to the prophetic message,
while the day dawns
and the morning star rises in our heart.[9]

~

Through Jesus and through grace
may we know eternal comfort and hope
– our hearts strengthened in every good work and word.[10]

REFERENCES
1) Rom. 8:24, 25
2) Rom. 4:18
3) Rom. 15:13
4) Rom. 5:1, 2
5) Rom. 15:4
6) Col. 1:26, 27
7) 1 John 3:2, 3
8) Heb. 6:18–20
9) 2 Pet. 1:19
10) 2 Thess. 2:16, 17

47.   *Hospitality*

'I was hungry and you gave me food;
thirsty and you gave me drink.'
'Come and inherit the kingdom,
you, whom my Father has blessed.'[1]

~

For many will come from the east and the west,
from the north and the south they will come.
They will eat in the kingdom, the kingdom of God
– hospitality unending.[2]

~

Make our giving generous, God, ready to meet all needs,
extending hospitality to enemy, to stranger,
according to the gifts you have given.[3]

~

Like the Samaritan, bandaging wounds,
pouring in oil and wine
or Zaccheus descending in haste from the tree
in response to the call of Jesus.[4 & 5]

~

This is my blood, poured out for many,
the blood of the new covenant.
This is my body, take and eat,
may our hospitality be Eucharist.[6]

~

Let us be one with the crippled, the poor,
the blind, the rejected, the lame.
Inviting, celebrating, ministering with all
in mutual love and service.[7]

~

Remembering prisoners and those who are tortured,
as though we too were unfree.
Walking with them and bearing their pain
– one body in Christ are we.[8]

~

Serving one another as stewards of grace,
enabling constant love
love that covers many a sin –
– hospitality, uncomplaining.[9]

~

Like the disciples we invite Christ to stay
for the day is now nearly spent.
Renew our faith, Jesus,
make holy our welcoming.
Blessed by your Father are we.[10]

REFERENCES
1) Matt. 25:35, 34
2) Luke 13:29
3) Rom. 12:6–20
4) Luke 10:29–37
5) Luke 19:6
6) Mark 14:22–25
7) Luke 14:16–21
8) Heb. 13:1–3
9) 1 Pet. 4:8–10
10) Luke 24:28–32

48. *Immortality*

God, you are rich in mercy.
You loved us totally even when dead through our sins
and brought us to life, together with Christ.
By grace we have been saved.[1]

~

If our hope in Christ were for this life only,
most pitiable indeed would we be
but as all people died in Adam,
so all will be made alive in Christ.[2]

~

Jesus is the resurrection and the life
and all who live and believe in him will never die.[3]

~

For this perishable body will put on imperishability
and this mortal body will be clothed in immortality –
thus death will be swallowed up in victory.[4]

~

For, dwelling within us is God's own spirit,
giving life to our mortal bodies
– God who raised Jesus from the dead.[5]

~

Like Paul, we experience the suffering of Christ
– Christ living in us,
living by faith in the Son of God
who loved and gave himself for us.[6]

Let us long for the appearing of the righteous judge
who will give the crown of righteousness
to those who have walked with others in their need,
to all who have desired his coming.[7]

REFERENCES
1) Eph. 2:4, 5
3) John 11:24–26
5) Rom. 8:11
7) 2 Tim. 4:8

2) 1 Cor. 15:19–22
4) 1 Cor. 15:54, 55
6) 2 Cor. 1:5

49.   *John the Baptizer*

God, in the wilderness of our world,
may our message be:
'repent for the kingdom of heaven is near'.[1]
~

Let our lives be in keeping with what we proclaim,
our fruits worthy of repentance.[2]
~

Our mission is prophet, messenger and herald,
preparing the way for Jesus.[3]
~

Sent by you we witness to the light
that through us all might believe.[4]
~

Let ours be the voice crying out on the earth:
Here is the Lamb of God; he forgives the sin of the world.
Make straight the way for him.[5]
~

Give us the courage the Baptist showed
in upholding goodness and right.[6]
~

May we be a burning and shining lamp,
testifying ever to truth.[7]
~

As the Spirit descended on Jesus your Son,
we too are baptized in the Spirit.
With John we make our prayer of faith:
This is the Son of God.[8]

~

Unworthy are we to loose Jesus' sandal.[9]
We know we are not the Messiah;[10]
simply a voice, missioned and sent
to give the good news of the Kingdom.[11]

REFERENCES
1) Matt. 3:2
2) Matt. 3:8
3) Matt. 11:10
4) John 1:6–8
5) John 1:23–29
6) Matt. 14:4–12
7) John 5:35
8) John 1:33, 34
9) John 1:27
10) John 1:20
11) John 1:23

50. *Joseph*

Generations have passed and the time has now come.
Joseph, guardian of God's only Son.[1]

~

Joseph, son of David, do not be afraid.
Mary has conceived by God's Holy Spirit.[2]

~

In our times of anguish, confusion and doubt,
we relate with the agony in Joseph's own heart.[3]

~

With love we all grieve with Joseph and Mary
– no room at the inn; only a stable.[4]

~

Let us haste with the shepherds and ponder anew
– Mary and Joseph, the child Jesus too.[5]

~

God is with us – Emmanuel.
The words of the prophet are now fulfilled.[6]

~

A pair of turtle doves, the gift of the poor.
Yet, the name of Jesus means Saviour of all.[7]

~

With authority invested in him and true to the angel's
      word,
Joseph proclaimed the child's name
– Jesus, Saviour of the world.[8]

We pray for the trust and detachment of Joseph,
trudging at night into Egypt.
And when danger had ceased and the order was given,
returning with Mary and Jesus.[9]

~

Joseph the righteous, guardian of Jesus,
his teacher, confidant and friend,
be with us as we walk the journey of life
and lead us, in faith, to the end.[10]

REFERENCES
1) Matt. 1:16, 17
2) Matt. 1:18–22
3) Matt. 1:19, 20
4) Luke 2:4–7
5) Luke 2:15, 16
6) Matt. 1:22, 23
7) Luke 2:22–32
8) Luke 2:21
9) Matt. 2:13–15, 19–23
10) Matt. 1:16–25; Luke 2:51

51. *Journey of Life*

God, as Jesus your Son came into the world,
we too experience life's journeying.
May we be ready at our journey's end
to leave the world and go to you.[1]

~

You are the one who sent your Son
and left him not alone.
Be with us as you send each one.
Walk with us on our journey.[2]

~

May we have the confidence, the trust of Jesus,
thanking you, God, for hearing us.
We know that you always hear us.[3]

~

In love, God, show us all that you are doing.
As we journey, show us even greater things.
We wonder at your power.[4]

~

We wish to know you as Jesus does,
for we also are from you
and you have sent us.[5]

~

We have made your name known to many
and will continue our journey to make you known,
so that the love with which you love us
may be in them.[6]

~

When we meet the cup of suffering
and from us it cannot pass,
let us embrace it with open hands.
Your will be done, our God.[7]

~

Make us one with your command
that the world may know our love for you,
for to glorify ourselves means nothing.
It is you who will glorify us.[8]

~

With Jesus, we desire to be with you,
for you loved us before the foundation of the world.
Show us, one day, your glory.[9]

REFERENCES
1) John 16:28
2) John 8:29
3) John 11:42
4) John 5:20
5) John 7:29
6) John 17:25, 26
7) Matt. 26:42; John 14:31
8) John 8:54
9) John 17:24

52. *Joy*

Our souls magnify the Lord
and our spirits rejoice in God our saviour.[1]

~

The word leaps joyfully in the depths of our being
at the sound of your voice.[2]

~

Good news and great joy for all people –
a Saviour, the Messiah is ours.
Fear? Never![3]

~

Overwhelmed with joy are our hearts
at the star brilliantly settled – its journey done.[4]

~

Though not seeing, we love,
though unbeholding, we believe
and a joy indescribable and glorious
wells forth in our hearts
– the outcome of our faith,
the salvation of our souls.[5]

~

Spirit of God, birth in us your fruits
– love, peace, joy.[6]

~

Rising above opposition,
lead us into godliness,
joyfully open to your word of life.[7]

~

For the kingdom is not food and drink
but righteousness, peace and joy in you.[8]

~

May the God of hope fill us
with all joy and peace in believing.
And by the power of his Spirit,
may our hearts abound in hope.[9]

REFERENCES
1) Luke 1:46, 47
2) Luke 1:43, 44
3) Luke 2:10, 11
4) Matt. 2:10
5) 1 Pet. 1:8, 9
6) Gal. 5:22
7) 1 Thess. 1:6
8) Rom. 14:17
9) Rom. 15:13

53.   *The Kingdom*

God in heaven, may your name be kept holy
as we await the coming of your kingdom.[1]
~

Detach us from unnecessary things
while sharing with the poor and needy.[2]
~

It is your pleasure to give us the kingdom.
'Never fear, little flock,' says Jesus.[3]
~

Like Jesus, let us proclaim the good news of the kingdom
– a kingdom that cannot be shaken.
Rendering thanks with reverence and awe,
our worship – acceptable.[4]
~

The poor of the world are the heirs of the kingdom,
those rich in faith and love.
Bring us to poorness in spirit, God,
that we may be chosen and blessed.[5]
~

For righteousness, peace and joy in the Spirit,
these are the signs of the kingdom.[6]
~

Let us live lives worthy of God
who calls us into his kingdom, his glory.[7]
~

Like little children owning our helplessness,
trusting totally and eager to receive.[8]

~

We thank you, God, for rescuing us from the power
  of darkness
and transferring us into the kingdom of your Son,
  the beloved,
in whom we are redeemed and forgiven.[9]

REFERENCES

1) Matt. 6:9, 10
2) Matt. 19:21
3) Luke 12:32
4) Matt. 4:23; Heb. 12:28
5) Jas 2:5
6) Rom. 14:17
7) 2 Thess. 1:11, 12
8) Matt. 18:2–4
9) Col. 1:13, 14

54. *Leadership*

You ought to wash one another's feet.
I have set you an example.[1]
~

Help us, God, to see leadership as service,
remembering to be first is also to be slave.[2]
~

As servants of Christ we are stewards of your mysteries.
We want to be trustworthy in your sight, our God.[3]
~

Make us hospitable, lovers of goodness,
prudent, upright and self-controlled.[4]
~

Give us eagerness in tending your flock,
not lording it over them, but being examples.[5]
~

Commissioned by you, God, we are servants of
   the church.
Let us make your word known in all its fullness.[6]
~

May no greater joy be ours than this:
that all our children are walking in the truth.[7]
~

As your servants, God, help us be kindly,
teaching with patience, correcting in gentleness.[8]
~

We know that suffering must be endured
as we carry out our ministry, proclaiming the word.[9]

~

The authority you give is for building up each one.
May we never be ashamed of our trust.[10]

REFERENCES

1) John 13:12–15
3) 1 Cor. 4:1, 2
5) 1 Pet. 5:1–3
7) 3 John 4
9) 2 Tim. 4:1–5

2) Matt. 20:25–28
4) Titus 1:8
6) Col. 1:24–26
8) 2 Tim. 2:24–26
10) 2 Cor. 10:8

55. *Life*

God of immortality, dwelling in unapproachable light,
to you be honour and eternal dominion.[1]
~

In your great mercy you have given us a new birth in a
    living hope,
by raising your Son, Jesus, from the dead.[2]
~

Jesus, you are the resurrection and the life.
Deepen our faith in you that we may live.[3]
~

Let us live to you, God,
let us die to you
that we may truly belong to you
– God of the living and the dead.[4]
~

Make us gospel people, righteous, faith-filled,
for those who are righteous will live by faith.[5]
~

Remembering your own spirit dwells within us,
giving life to our mortal bodies
your Spirit, who raised Jesus from the dead.[6]
~

Let us take hold of the eternal life to which we are called.
Let us witness to this calling in the presence of all.[7]
~

Set our minds, God, on things that are above,
our life hidden with Christ in you – Christ our life,
with whom we will be revealed in glory.[8]

~

By baptism into Christ
we were baptized into his death
and by his resurrection to glory.
We can now walk in newness of life.[9]

~

By his death, Christ died to sin
but the life he lives, he lives to God.
Let us then be dead to sin
and alive to God, in Jesus.[10]

REFERENCES
1) 1 Tim 6:16
2) 1 Pet. 1:3
3) John 11:25, 26
4) Rom. 14:7–9
5) Rom. 1:17
6) Rom. 8:11
7) 1 Tim. 6:12
8) Col. 3:2–4
9) Rom 6:3, 4
10) Rom. 6:10, 11

56. *Light*

Your Son Jesus, God, came into the world
to draw us from darkness into light.[1]
~
Guide our footsteps, lighting our way,
that darkness may never overtake us.[2]
~
Strengthen among us our togetherness,
walking in Jesus, the Light.[3]
~
For the people in darkness saw a great light
and the shadow of death transformed.[4]
~
And the eyes of Simeon saw your salvation
– for Israel, glory
– for the Gentiles, a light.[5]
~
Jesus' face shone like the sun,
his garments dazzling white.[6]
~
We thank you, God, for enabling us to share
in the inheritance of the saints in light.[7]
~
A light that has made us a holy people,
a royal priesthood, a chosen race.[8]
~

And the fruits of the light are to be found
in goodness, justice and right.[9]

~

You have shone in our hearts.
May our light shine forth.
To you be the praise and the glory.[10]

REFERENCES
1) John 12:46
3) 1 John 1:5–7
5) Luke 2:30–32
7) Col. 1:11–14
9) Eph. 5:8, 9

2) John 12:35, 36
4) Matt. 4:13–16
6) Matt. 17:2
8) 1 Pet. 2:9
10) 2 Cor. 4:4–6; Matt. 5:14–16

57. *Listening*

We thank you, God, for the gift of faith
that came to us through hearing Christ's word.[1]

~

Gift each of us with a listening heart
and deepen in us the understanding that your
    Spirit gives.[2]

~

Let us be generous in sharing faith,
telling one another what we hear and see.[3]

~

May hearts that are dull and ears deaf with hardening
become open to your healing power.[4]

~

Keep us always united in faith,
listening and receiving the message of Jesus.[5]

~

Always aware of your voice from the cloud:
'This is my Son, the Beloved; listen to him.'[6]

~

Remembering we have received grace and apostleship
to bring about the obedience of faith.[7]

~

Send forth your Spirit anew to our world
that all nations may see and hear.[8]

~

In obedience to the truth, may our lives be pure,
growing in genuine, mutual love.[9]

~

May your word be at work in all believers,
enabling acceptance in depth.
For the word we accepted is no human word.
It is God's word at work in us.[10]

REFERENCES
1) Rom. 10:16, 17
3) Matt. 11:4, 5
5) Heb. 4:1, 2
7) Rom 1:3–5
9) 1 Pet. 1:22

2) Matt. 13:14, 15
4) Heb. 3:8–10
6) Mark 9:7
8) Acts 2:17–21
10) 1 Thess. 2:13

58.   *Loving God in Others*

God, you have given us through Jesus a new
      commandment.
Help us to love one another as Jesus has loved us.[1]
~

By the love we have for one another
let us be recognized as disciples of Jesus.[2]
~

Grace us to rejoice when others rejoice
and to be sad with those in sorrow.[3]
~

Make our world one group of believers,
united like the early Christians in heart and soul.[4]
~

Knowing we can have no greater love
than to lay down our lives for our friends.[5]
~

According to the grace that was given to each,
let us use our gifts in service,
aiming to be rich in all those gifts
which go to build up the community.[6]
~

Love is the greatest of all the gifts
– patient, kind, rejoicing in the truth,
ready to make allowances,
to endure whatever comes.
Love never comes to an end.[7]

~

Spirit of God, make firm our inner selves.
May Christ live in our hearts through faith
that we may be planted in love and built on love.[8]

~

Remembering what we do to the least of your people,
to you, God, it is also done.[9]

~

For the sake of your glory
let us accept one another,
as Christ has accepted us.[10]

REFERENCES
1) John 13:34   2) John 13:35
3) Rom. 12:10   4) Acts 4:32
5) John 15:13   6) 1 Cor. 12:4–11; 14:26
7) 1 Cor. 13:4–8, 13   8) Eph. 3:16–19
9) Matt. 25:33–40   10) Rom. 15:7

59. *Magdalen*

We thank you, God, for your grace in Magdalen,
cleansing her to love you as she did.[1]
~
May we follow you to Calvary, in love,
as Mary and the other women did.[2]
~
Gift us with her repentant love,
she who came to the tomb with sadness and hope.[3]
~
As she wept, seeing the emptiness there,
may we also weep when Jesus seems absent.[4]
~
Jesus, we know you call us by name.
May we behold you in every person.[5]
~
And make strong our hope in our own resurrection
so that we too can say 'We have seen the Lord.'[6]
~
When disbelief is the response to our words,
keep us firm and steeped in faith.
With courage, overcoming all human respect
and making concrete our good intentions.[7]
~
Through the loyalty of Magdalen who stood by the cross,
may our faith and trust endure to the end.[8]

When asked at death 'Who do you seek?'
The risen Christ! Our joy complete.[9]

REFERENCES

1) Luke 8:1, 2
2) Matt. 27:56
3) John 20:1
4) John 20:11–15
5) John 20:16
6) John 20:18
7) Luke 24:9–11
8) John 19:25
9) John 20:15

60. *Marriage*

God, lead us to hold in high honour your gift of marriage
– pure the marriage bed.[1]

~

For you created male and female,
husband and wife living together as one.
A union so sacred, inseparable.[2]

~

Just as woman came from man
so man came through woman,
each dependent on the other
but all things come from God.[3]

~

Enable husbands to love their wives
and to treat them with gentleness,[4]
loving them as Christ loved the Church
and gave himself up for her.[5]

~

Enable wives to respect their husbands[6]
and deepen the awareness of each
to the other's needs and limitations.
Remembering that both are heirs
to the gracious gift of life.[7]

~

Make their homes, God, places of welcome
like the warm hospitality of Martha.[8]

And may their children increase in wisdom and years, in divine and human favour.[9]

REFERENCES
1) Heb. 13:4
3) 1 Cor. 11, 12
5) Eph. 5:25
7) 1 Pet. 3:7
9) Luke 2:52

2) Matt. 19:4–6
4) Col. 3:19
6) Eph. 5:33
8) Luke 10:38

61. *Mary*

'Greetings, favoured one! The Lord is with you.'
'The power of the Most High will overshadow you.'[1]

~

God, give us the faith of Mary who believed.
Renew us, like Elizabeth, with the fullness of your Spirit.[2]

~

'The Word became flesh and lived among us.'
May all hearts be open to receive him anew.[3]

~

Like Mary's child, Jesus, may all children grow strong,
filled with wisdom and enjoying your favour.[4]

~

In times of anxiety and failure to understand,
let us treasure, like Mary, your word in our hearts.[5]

~

Mary, you have been given to us.
May we, like John, take you into our home.[6]

~

We remember your words spoken at Cana:
'Do whatever he tells you.'[7]

~

When trial and suffering are part of our life,
help us to bear the sword that pierces.[8]

~

As Mary tended your needs with love,
help us, Jesus, in our caring.[9]

~

And with Mary, present in the early Church,
let our prayer and action be holy.[10]

REFERENCES
1) Luke 1:28–35
3) John 1:14
5) Luke 2:42–52
7) John 2:1–11
9) John 19:23, 24

2) Luke 1:39–45
4) Luke 2:40
6) John 19:26, 27
8) Luke 2:34, 35
10) Acts 1:14

62. *Meals*

Jesus, you gave the first of your signs
at the wedding feast of Cana.[1]

~

You joined in the banquet given by Levi,
accepting all who were present.[2]

~

In compassion you shared the loaves and the fish.
The people all ate and were filled.[3]

~

Forgiveness was given and a woman loved
in the Pharisee's house at table.[4]

~

Taking the bread, you broke it.
Taking the cup, you gave thanks.
This is my body, given for you.
My blood, poured out for many.[5]

~

You asked for a drink at Jacob's well
and spoke of the water of life.[6]
And joined in the dinner served by Martha
at the home of your Bethany friends.[7]

~

Your disciples, disbelieving and wondering still,
saw you eat in their presence.[8]

~

And you opened the eyes of the travellers to Emmaus,
at table – breaking bread.[9]

~

The breakfast you served from the charcoal fire
was enjoyed by your weary disciples.

~

Let us cherish our times of leisure and quiet,
our times for eating and rest.[10]

~

And blessed are we if we hear God's words:
'Come to the Lamb's Wedding Feast.'[11]

REFERENCES

1) John 2:1–11
2) Luke 5:29
3) Luke 9:12–17
4) Luke 7:36–50
5) Luke 22:14–20
6) John 4:7–14
7) John 12:1, 2
8) Luke 24:41–43
9) Luke 24:30, 31
10) John 21:3–8; Mark 6:31, 32
11) Rev. 19:9

63. *Mercy*

God, we know that our hearts must always forgive,
not seven times only, but again and again.[1]

~

A repentant heart must always be forgiven.
Give us grace to respond to the asking.[2]

~

Your mercy is from generation to generation
for those who revere you.
May we always know your mercy.[3]

~

Help us to bear with one another in our weakness
and to forgive, just as we have received your forgiveness.[4]

~

We thank you, God, for rescuing us from the power
    of darkness,
and transferring us into the Kingdom of the Son
    you love.
In him we have redemption – our sins forgiven.[5]

~

By your tender mercy, God,
the dawn from on high has visited us.[6]

~

Make us perfect in merciful loving.
As you, God of heaven, are perfect.[7]

~

May we, like the Baptist, prepare the way
so that all can know your forgiveness
and experience your salvation.[8]

~

We ask that we be among the blessed
that we may receive mercy.[9]

REFERENCES
1) Matt. 18:21, 22
2) Luke 17:4
3) Luke 1:50
4) Col. 3:13
5) Col. 1:13, 14
6) Luke 1:78–79
7) Matt. 5:48
8) Luke 1:76–78
9) Matt. 5:7

64. *Miracle*

God, give us the faith that enables miracles.
You healed the paralytic through the faith of his friends.[1]

~

Help us in accepting whatever you plan.
The leper was cured – he left all in your hands.[2]

~

Let us step out in faith, with absolute trust,
walking, like Jesus, the waters of life.[3]

~

And never allow others to struggle in pain
because of our absence or weakness of faith.[4]

~

May we know, God, your presence midst the noise of
  our world.
Like the blind man of Jericho; you will hear and
  have pity.[5]

~

Make radical our faith, Jesus.
Give us the courage of the woman who touched the
  fringe of your cloak.[6]

~

The five thousand were fed with love and compassion.
May we always be ready to share what we have.[7]

~

In total humility, like the Canaanite woman,
let us own our weakness and accept all as gift.[8]

~

Deepen in us, God, the freedom of Jesus.
May we not be enslaved by the letter of the law.[9]

~

And like the Centurion who loved his servant,
make us deeply aware that all life is sacred.[10]

REFERENCES
1) Matt. 9:1–8
3) Matt. 14:22–33
5) Matt. 20:29–34
7) Matt. 14:13–21
9) Matt. 12:9–14

2) Matt. 8:1–4
4) Matt. 17:14–20
6) Matt. 9:18–26
8) Matt. 15:22–28
10) Matt. 8:5–13

65. *Mission*

God, give us grace to accept your plan,
courage to carry out our mission.[1]

~

Like the Baptist, a voice crying out in the wilderness,
let us help all people to see your salvation.[2]

~

Jesus, you brought the good news to the poor,
release to the captives and sight to the blind.
Empower us to let the oppressed go free,
to proclaim to all people a time of God's favour.[3]

~

Let us hear, once again, your words – 'follow me'.
Deepen our commitment to mission.[4]

~

Leaving anew all that we have
– ready for total giving.[5]

~

Call us each moment to be your disciples,
sending us out to proclaim the message.[6]

~

With Peter, let us say: 'To whom can we go?
You have the words of eternal life.'[7]

~

You have shone in our hearts, God,
and given us the knowledge of your own glory,
in the face of Jesus.[8]

REFERENCES
1) Luke 1:31–38; Matt. 1:18–24   2) John 1:19–23
3) Luke 4:17–21   4) Luke 5:27–29; 4:18–22
5) Matt. 4:21, 22   6) Mark 16:15
7) John 6:67–69   8) 2 Cor. 4:5, 6

66. *Motherhood*

God, in motherliness, gather your children
as a hen gathers her brood beneath her wings.[1]

~

Send your Holy Spirit upon all mothers.
Overshadow them with your power.[2]

~

Deepen their faith and make it sincere
like the faith of their mothers before them.[3]

~

Give them fidelity in their suffering
when pierced with the sword of pain.[4]

~

Bless their generosity in times of struggle,
as they share the little they have.[5]

~

And hear their pleas for your healing touch
for children sick and ailing.[6]

~

Walk with mothers in times of loss,
gently easing their grieving.[7]

~

Temper their ambition and keep them from evil.
Draw them to deeper conversion.[8]

~

Help mothers cherish their children as gifts:
ready are they for the Kingdom.[9]

~

And deepen our reverence for the sacredness of life,
knowing you are the God of all.[10]

REFERENCES
1) Luke 13:34
2) Luke 1:35
3) 2 Tim. 1:5
4) Luke 2:33–35; John 19:25
5) Luke 21:1–4
6) Mark 7:24–30
7) Luke 7:11–15
8) Matt. 20:20–22
9) Luke 18:15, 16
10) Luke 1:24, 25

67. *Obedience*

God, your Son, Jesus, came into this world to carry out
   your will.
And so, through the offering of his body for all
we have now been sanctified.[1]

~

Jesus, you spoke of God's will as food.
Sustain us as we work.
Nourish our resolve to do God's will,
God's teaching, not our own.[2]

~

We will never be lost or forgotten,
for to Jesus we have been given.
Let us see your Son, God, we believe in him.
Raise us to life eternal.[3]

~

We know that Jesus' obedience to you
was the source of his power to act.
Empower us, God, with your own Spirit.
Draw us to oneness of will.[4]

~

Let our minds be the same as the mind of Christ Jesus
– a total emptying of self,
obedient to death, death on a cross.
May his dying be our strength.[5]

~

I do nothing on my own, said Jesus,
only as the Father has told me.
God, bring our wills into harmony with yours,
even on our way to Gethsemane.[6]

~

Through our pain may we learn obedience,
submitting in reverence and in trust.[7]
'Not my will but yours be done'
– two wills merging as one.[8]

~

Like Jesus, you never leave us alone.
May we do what is pleasing to you,[9]
glorifying you by completing our mission
the work you give us to do.[10]

REFERENCES
1) Heb. 10:5–10
3) John 6:38–40
5) Phil. 2:5–8
7) Heb. 5:7, 8
9) John 8:28, 29

2) John 4:34; 7:16, 17
4) Matt. 8:9
6) John 5:30; 14:31
8) Luke 22:42
10) John 17:4

68.   *Patience*

Spirit of God, nurture within us your fruits
– love, peace, patience.[1]

~

As your holy ones, beloved and chosen,
clothe us with patience in bearing with one another.[2]

~

We want to live lives worthy of our calling,
with humility, gentleness and patience.[3]

~

As the farmer waits for the crop to grow
and patiently hopes for early and late rains,
give us the grace to wait in patience
for the day of your own coming.[4]

~

With you, God, a thousand years are like a single day.
Be patient with us and with our world,
enabling salvation for everyone.[5]

~

Make us strong with the strength of your power
that we may endure everything with patience.[6]

~

Imitating those who through faith and patience
are able to inherit the promises.[7]

~

Never despising the riches of God's kindness
– goodness, forbearance and patience.[8]

~

In admonishing, encouraging and helping others,
gift us with patience for all.[9]

~

And steep us in Jesus' own patience towards us,
on our journey to life eternal.[10]

REFERENCES
1) 1 Cor. 13:4
2) Col. 3:12, 13
3) Eph. 4:1–3
4) Jas. 5:7–11
5) 2 Pet. 3:8, 9
6) Col. 1:11, 12
7) Heb. 6:11, 12
8) Rom. 2:1–7
9) 1 Thess. 5:14
10) 1 Tim. 1:16

69. *Paul*

'Who are you Lord?' asked the shattered Saul.
'I am Jesus whom you are persecuting.'[1]
~

Paul, servant of God and apostle of Christ,
shares with us the grace and peace he has received.[2]
~

With Paul, we remember and pray for one another,
giving thanks to God for the joy we share.[3]
~

Help us, God, to become all things to all people,
that they may partake of the blessings of the Gospel.[4]
~

May we strengthen one another with some spiritual gift
and yearn like Paul for the sharing of our faith.[5]
~

We know that Christ Jesus has made us his own
and we strain towards the goal to which we are called.[6]
~

Carrying in our bodies the death of Jesus,
so that his life too may be visible in us[7]
for the tent we now live in will be destroyed
and we long to be clothed with our heavenly dwelling.[8]
~

And so we come to regard all things as loss,
because of the value of knowing Christ Jesus.[9]

~

When the time draws near for us to be gone,
may we also with Paul have kept the faith.[10]

REFERENCES

1) Acts 9:5   2) Titus 1:1–4
3) Phil. 1:3   4) 1 Cor. 9:19–23
5) Rom. 1:11, 12   6) Phil. 3:12–16
7) 2 Cor. 4:10   8) 2 Cor. 5:1–3
9) Phil. 3:8   10) 2 Tim. 4:6–8

70.   *Peace*

You have called us, God, to peace
– peace with one another.[1]

~

Enable Christ's peace to reign in our hearts
for to this we are called in one body.[2]

~

Let us then seek peace and pursue it ever,
for our God is a God of peace.[3]

~

It is through Jesus that we have peace with you,
for he, the Christ, is our peace.[4]

~

May we be entirely one new humanity
– sanctified, reconciled, at peace.[5]

~

For your kingdom, God, is not food and drink
but righteousness and peace in the Spirit.[6]

~

Let us be peacemakers, children of God,
pursuing what makes for mutual up-building.[7]

~

Abounding in hope by the power of your spirit
may we know joy and peace in believing.[8]

~

Give to our world peace in abundance.
We long to be in Christ Jesus.[9]

~

Jesus, you have given your peace to us.
May we never be afraid or troubled.[10]

REFERENCES

1) 1 Cor. 7:15; Mark 9:50
2) Col. 3:15
3) 1 Pet. 3:11; 1 Cor. 14:33
4) Rom. 5:1, 2; Eph. 2:14
5) Eph. 2:15–18; 1 Thess. 5:23
6) Rom. 14:17
7) Matt. 5:9; Rom. 14:19
8) Rom. 15:13
9) Jude vv. 1, 2; 1 Pet. 5:14
10) John 14:27

71.   *Perseverance*

Enabling God, you know our weakness
and the test will never be beyond our strength.[1]

~

As Jesus suffered and left an example,
give us strength to follow his steps.[2]

~

Support us in every hardship, God,
that we in turn may support one another.[3]

~

Preaching Jesus – a crucified Christ
but also the power and the wisdom of God.[4]

~

Give us perseverance; deepen our faith
that we may be worthy of your own kingdom.[5]

~

Remembering that if we have died with Jesus
we shall live with him
and if we have endured with Jesus,
we shall also reign with him.[6]

~

For Christ suffered once for all the world's sin
that he might lead all people to you.[7]

~

As Jesus, the innocent, died for all,
may our life be upright: may we die to our sins.[8]

Increase our trust as you allow us to suffer,
witnessing always to the suffering of Christ.[9]

~

With the sufferings we bear, encouragement we share,
in this knowledge, God, may our hope be secure.[10]

REFERENCES

1) 1 Cor. 10:13

2) 1 Pet. 2:21

3) 2 Cor. 1:4

4) 1 Cor. 1:22–24

5) 2 Thess. 1:4, 5

6) 2 Tim. 2:11, 12

7) 1 Pet. 3:18

8) 1 Pet. 2:20–25

9) 1 Pet. 4:12–19

10) 2 Cor. 1:7

72.   *Peter*

God, after the example of Peter and the apostles
let us leave anew what we have and follow Jesus.[1]

~

Set our minds on the things that are divine
– not on human things.[2]

~

Deepen the little faith that we have.
We know Jesus is truly your Son.[3]

~

Strengthen our weakness, make willing our spirit
to watch and pray in times of distress.[4]

~

Bring us, like Peter, to own our sinfulness
as we stand in awe at your wonders.[5]

~

With him we make our profession of faith:
Jesus has the words of eternal life.
He is the holy one in whom we believe.
God, to whom else can we go?[6]

~

Jesus, take us to the mountain top;
give us a glimpse of your glory.
It is good for us to be here with you.
We long to remain in your presence.[7]

~

Gift us with total conversion of heart
as we weep for ourselves and our world.[8]

~

Confident in the healing power of your spirit,
may we reach out to those in affliction.[9]

~

Like Peter, unbind the chains that enslave us.
Open the gates to our freedom.[10]

REFERENCES

1) Matt. 4:18–20

3) Matt. 14:28–33

5) Luke 5:4–8

7) Matt. 17:1–4

9) Acts 3:6, 7

2) Matt. 16:21–23

4) Matt. 26:40, 41

6) John 6:66–69

8) Matt. 26:69–75

10) Acts 12:6–11

73.   *Possessions*

'Out of her poverty, she put in everything,
all she had to live on.'[1]
~

Bring us, God, to cheerfulness in giving,
sharing abundantly in every good work.[2]
~

You have given us your spirit and anointed us
to bring good news to the poor.[3]
~

For the poor we will always have with us.
They are blessed, for the kingdom is theirs.[4]
~

You look on us, Jesus, with deep love.
Make total our following of you.[5]
~

Ready us, God, to share our resources,
spiritual blessings and material things.[6]
~

Let us not worry about our life and its needs
but rather strive first for the kingdom.[7]
~

Put us on guard against all kinds of greed.
From abundance of possessions unclutter us.[8]
~

You have chosen us, God, as heirs to the kingdom.
Bring us to poorness – to richness in faith.[9]

~

May your love abide in our hearts we pray,
as we love in truth and action.[10]

REFERENCES

1) Mark 12:43–44

3) Luke 4:18

5) Mark 10:21, 22

7) Matt. 6:25–33

9) Jas 2:5

2) 2 Cor. 9:7–9

4) Mark 14:7; Luke 6:20

6) Rom. 15:25–27

8) Luke 12:15

10) 1 John 3:17–18

74.   *Prayer*

Holy Spirit, help us in our weakness.
You pray for us in accordance with the mind of God.[1]
~

While rejoicing in hope and patient in suffering,
grace us, God, to persevere in prayer.[2]
~

Help us to pray as your Son Jesus prayed:
Father, your name be hallowed.[3]
~

At all times praying in your Holy Spirit,
making supplication for all.[4]
~

In cheerfulness, singing songs of praise,
in sickness, the prayer of anointing,
praying with faith and for one another.
The prayer of the righteous is powerful.[5]
~

All your creation, God, is good.
Let us receive with thanksgiving
for all is sanctified by your word.
Be with us in our prayer.[6]
~

Devoting ourselves to the word and to fellowship,
to the breaking of bread and the prayers.[7]
~

If we ask, it will be given to us.
In searching we will find.
Knocking will open the door for us
– all in Jesus' name.[8]

~

We pray, God, that your word may spread,
that everywhere you may be glorified.[9]

~

May our prayer and alms ascend before you
and may the prayers of many bring blessings.[10]

REFERENCES
1) Rom. 8:26, 27
2) Rom. 12:13
3) Luke 11:1–4
4) Eph. 6:18; 1 Tim. 2:1, 2
5) Jas 5:13–16
6) 1 Tim. 4:4, 5
7) Acts 2:42
8) Matt. 7:7–11; John 14:13
9) 2 Thess. 3:1 ,2
10) 2 Cor. 1:11; Acts 10:31

75.   *Purity of Heart*

Let us walk in the light together with one another
and the blood of Jesus will cleanse us from all sin.[1]

~

Draw near to us, God, as we draw near to you.
Cleanse our hands and purify our hearts.[2]

~

You call us, not to impurity but to holiness.
May we never reject your authority
or the gift of your Holy Spirit.[3]

~

By obedience to the truth may our souls be purified
so that genuine mutual love may be ours.[4]

~

Purify our conscience from the dead works of sin.
Through the blood of Christ and the eternal Spirit,
may we offer worship to you.[5]

~

We want to be like you, our God,
when we see you as you are.
Purify us then, just as you are pure.[6]

~

Remembering we are children of light, of the day.
We are not of the night or of darkness.[7]

~

As though reflected in a mirror we see your glory, God.
Gently transform us into this same glory
through the power of your holy Spirit.[8]

~

May the cunning of evil never lead us astray.
Gift us with sincere and pure devotion to Christ.[9]

~

You have called us with a holy calling,
according to your own purpose and grace revealed
   in Jesus,
who abolished death and brought life and immortality
   to light.[10]

REFERENCES
1) 1 John 1:7
2) Jas 4:8
3) 1 Thess. 4:7, 8
4) 1 Pet. 1:22
5) Heb. 9:13, 14
6) 1 John 3:2, 3
7) 1 Thess. 5:4–8
8) 2 Cor. 3:18
9) 2 Cor. 11:3
10) 2 Tim. 1:8–10

Note: Biblical purity is single-mindedness in the search for God.

76.   *Reconciliation*

Even while we were enemies,
we were reconciled to you, God,
through the death of your Son.[1]
~

We thank you for reconciling all things to yourself,
things on earth and things in heaven,
making peace through the blood of Christ.[2]
~

Yes, truly we have known salvation
by the forgiveness of our sins,
and by your tender mercy, God,
the dawn from on high has broken upon us.[3]
~

Make us perfect in merciful loving,
just as you are merciful.[4]
~

You have rescued us from the power of darkness
and transferred us into the kingdom of your Son.[5]
~

We who were once estranged and hostile
are now reconciled.
Make steadfast our faith.[6]
~

Enable us, God, in our ministry of reconciliation
that we do not accept your grace in vain.[7]

~

Like Jesus, let us sympathize with human weakness,
Jesus who was tested in all ways like ourselves.[8]

~

Rejoicing in celebration when forgiveness is given,
when the lost are found and death becomes life.[9]

~

Remembering always that where sin increased,
grace abounded all the more.[10]

REFERENCES
1) Rom. 5:10
2) Col. 1:19, 20
3) Luke 1:76–78
4) Luke 6:36
5) Col. 1:13, 14
6) Col. 1:21–23
7) 2 Cor. 5:17–6:1
8) Heb. 4:15, 16
9) Luke 15:22–27
10) Rom. 5:20

77. *Redemption*

We bless you, God.
You looked on us with favour
and redeemed us through Jesus, a mighty saviour.[1]
~

The blessing of Abraham has come to us
and we have received the promise of the Spirit
  through you.[2]
~

Disregarding the shame, you endured the cross.
Help us, your disciples, to take up our cross,
to deny ourselves and to follow you.[3]
~

Bring each of us, God, to pray in truth:
With Christ I have been crucified,
and now, no longer do I live
but Christ lives in me.[4]
~

We have shared in your Holy Spirit
and tasted the goodness of the word.
Let us never fall away
and crucify again your Son Jesus, the Christ.[5]
~

By making peace through the blood of his cross
all things are now reconciled.
For the fullness of your Godhead dwelt in Jesus.
May we too dwell in him.[6]

~

Our ransom not with things that perish
– not with gold and silver,
but the precious blood of Jesus Christ,
the Lamb without spot or blemish.[7]

~

You have rescued us, God, from the power of darkness
and transferred us to the kingdom of your Son
– your Son, the beloved, in whom we are redeemed,
in whom we are forgiven.[8]

REFERENCES
1) Luke 1:68, 69   2) Gal. 3:14–18
3) Heb. 12:2; Matt. 16:24, 25   4) Gal. 2:20
5) Heb. 6:5, 6   6) Col. 1:19, 20
7) 1 Pet. 1:18, 19   8) Col. 1:13, 14

78. *Repentance*

The time is fulfilled,
and the Kingdom of God has come near;
repent and believe the Good News.[1]

~

Grace us, God; we need to change.
Gift us with childlike trust and surrender.[2]

~

Make generous our turning to you in love,
remembering you first turned to us.[3]

~

Let us proclaim, in your name, to all the nations
the message of repentance,
the forgiveness of sins.[4]

~

You exalted Jesus as Leader and Saviour,
that we might be gifted with repentance and forgiveness.[5]

~

Open our being to the Spirit of Jesus
that our world may become a converted people.[6]

~

A people turned from darkness to light,
from the power of Satan to the holiness of God,
placed among those who are sanctified by faith.[7]

~

That times of refreshing may come to us
from the presence of Jesus among us,
deepen our turning to you each day
as we move towards total sinlessness.[8]

~

Soften the hearts that are hard and impenitent.
May they realize your kindness will lead them.[9]

~

And fill, God, the void of human ignorance,
enabling repentance for all.[10]

REFERENCES
1) Mark 1:14, 15
2) Matt. 18:3, 4
3) 1 John 4:19
4) Luke 24:47
5) Acts 5:31
6) Luke 4:18
7) Acts 26:18
8) Acts 3:19, 20
9) Rom. 2:4, 5
10) Acts 17:30

79.   *Resurrection*

God, your Son Jesus, in accordance with your will
laid down his life to take it up again.[1]
~
We are witnesses to his resurrection as the first
    apostles were.
Grace us to proclaim Jesus, the risen Lord.[2]
~
You raised Jesus from death.
To be held in its power was impossible for him.[3]
~
Christ then, is the first fruit of our redemption.[4]
~
He is the head of the body, the Church;
the beginning, the first born from the dead.
First place is his – in everything.[5]
~
May we hand on to all what we have received:
Christ's death for our sins,
his rising the third day,
his appearance to the twelve
– the scriptures fulfilled.[6]
~
In baptism we were buried with Jesus
and through faith in God's power
we were also raised with him.[7]

As Christ was raised by the glory of the Father,
so we too might walk in newness of life.[8]

~

All we want is to know Christ and the power of
    his rising,
to share his sufferings,
become like him in his death,
that somehow we may attain resurrection.[9]

~

For, hearing the word through Jesus
and believing that God sent him
is our passage from death to life.[10]

REFERENCES

1) John 10:17, 18   2) Acts 1:22
3) Acts 2:23, 24   4) 1 Cor. 15:23
5) Col. 1:18   6) 1 Cor. 15:3–5
7) Col. 2:12   8) Rom. 6:3–6
9) Phil. 3:10, 11   10) John 5:24

80. *Sacrifice*

Our paschal Lamb, Christ, has been sacrificed.
Let us celebrate the festival with the unleavened bread of
    sincerity and truth.[1]
~

As beloved children let us be imitators of God
and live in love as Christ loved us.[2]
He gave himself up – a fragrant offering –
a sacrifice to you, God, for us.[3]
~

Let us offer our bodies as a living sacrifice,
holy, acceptable – our spiritual worship.[4]
~

Build us, God, into a spiritual house, a holy priesthood,
offering spiritual sacrifices acceptable to you through
    Christ.[5]
~

We know that you have removed all sin
by the sacrifice of Jesus, your Son.[6]
~

Grace us to do good and to share what we have.
Such sacrifices are pleasing to you.[7]
~

Through Jesus we continually offer a sacrifice of praise,
the fruit of lips that confess his name.[8]
~

May the gifts we send be a fragrant offering,
a sacrifice acceptable and pleasing.[9]

~

For you, God, will satisfy our every need
according to your riches in glory in Christ.[10]

REFERENCES

1) 1 Cor. 5:7, 8   2) Eph. 5:1, 2
3) Eph. 5: 1, 2   4) Rom. 12:1
5) 1 Pet. 2:4, 5   6) Heb. 9:26
7) Heb. 13:16   8) Heb. 13:15
9) Eph. 5:2   10) Phil. 4:19

81. *Salvation*

Salvation belongs to our God who is seated on the
    throne
and to the Lamb.[1]

~

God, you have looked favourably on us your people
and redeemed us.[2]

~

Send us to give knowledge of salvation to your people
by the forgiveness of their sins.[3]

~

For we know that if we lose our life for your sake and
    the gospel
we will save it.[4]

~

We have been justified by the blood of Jesus
and in hope we are saved.[5]

~

He will transform our humble bodies and conform them
    to the body of his glory.
Our citizenship is in heaven.[6]

~

We have heard the word of truth, the gospel of our
    salvation;
been marked with the seal of the Holy Spirit,
the pledge of our inheritance.[7]

Acknowledging all as your gift to us, by grace we have
   been saved.[8]

~

We rejoice with a joy indescribable and glorious
– the outcome of our faith, the salvation of our souls.[9]

~

As we wait for the promised new heaven and new earth,
let us be found at peace without spot or blemish,
regarding the patience of our God as salvation.[10]

REFERENCES
1) Rev. 7:9, 10
3) Luke 1:77
5) Rom. 5:9; 8:24
7) Eph. 1:13, 14
9) 1 Pet. 1:8, 9

2) Luke 1:68, 69
4) Mark 8:35
6) Phil. 3:20, 21
8) Eph. 2:5–9
10) 2 Pet. 3:13–15

82. *Self-Transcendence*

God, out of your love for me
free me from attachment to life.[1]

~

As you gently invite me to restful quiet,
from the lure of activity free me.[2]

~

In moments of suffering, doubt and pain,
merge self-concern into grief for another.[3]

~

Unclutter my life of material things,
enabling greater likeness to Jesus.[4]

~

From resentment and unforgiveness,
heal me, God, that I may call the other 'friend'.[5]

~

All people are equal in your sight.
Cleanse my heart of racist tendencies.[6]

~

'Power' for Christ meant 'enablement'.
Let me never see power as dominance.[7]

~

In the courage of your Spirit, may I live out my mission
in spite of all threats and intimidation.[8]

~

That I may grow into the sinless Christ,
touch me in my sinfulness.[9]

REFERENCES

1) John 10:17, 18
2) Mark 6:30, 31
3) John 19:26, 27
4) Luke 9:58
5) Matt. 26:49, 50
6) John 4:9
7) John 6:15
8) Luke 13:31, 32
9) John 8:46

83. *Sharing*

God, in sharing with us your glory through Jesus,
may we be one as you and he are one.[1]
~

Share with us anew the grace of Jesus, your own love,
    God,
and the communion of your Spirit.[2]
~

Keep us from the corruption that is in the world
as we become participants in your divine nature.[3]
~

Make us eager to share what we have.
Such sacrifices are pleasing to you.[4]
~

Let us see our sharing as truly a privilege,
grateful for everything as a gift.[5]
~

We want to become all things to all people,
for the sake of the gospel
and to share in its blessings.[6]
~

In the blood of Jesus, we share.
We share in the body of Christ.
One bread, one body, in Eucharist we partake.[7]
~

If we have died with Jesus, we shall also live with him
and if we endure, we will reign
to share in his resurrection.[8]

~

Bring us to know Christ and the power of his rising,
to share in his sufferings, become like him in his death.[9]

~

We pray that the sharing of our faith be effective,
perceiving all the good we may do for Christ.[10]

REFERENCES

1) John 17:21, 22

2) 2 Cor. 13:13

3) 2 Pet. 1:4

4) 2 Cor. 8:3, 4

5) Heb. 13:16

6) 1 Cor. 9:22

7) 1 Cor. 10:16, 17

8) 2 Tim. 2:11–13

9) Phil 3:10

10) Philem. v. 6

84. *Simplicity*

God, we are like sheep in the midst of wolves.
Make us as wise as serpents and as simple as doves.[1]

~

Keep us chaste with the spiritual virginity of single-
    mindedness,
with a sincere and pure devotion to Christ.[2]

~

Change us, God, to become like children.
Make us humble that we may enter the kingdom.[3]

~

In welcoming those who are least among all – they are
    the greatest,
we welcome you, God.[4]

~

We do not celebrate with the yeast of malice
but with the unleavened bread of sincerity and truth.[5]

~

Speaking as persons of sincerity in Christ,
sent by you, God, we stand in your presence.[6]

~

Let us behave with frankness and godly sincerity
not by earthly wisdom but by your grace.[7]

~

Rid us, God, of all malice and guile,
all envy, insincerity and anger.
Longing for the pure, spiritual milk
that enables growth into salvation.[8]

~

Indeed our heart is in the testimony of our conscience.
May we never become false, deceitful, disguised.[9]

~

Open our hearts to embrace everyone.
May their hearts be open to receive our affection.[10]

REFERENCES
1) Matt. 10:16
2) 2 Cor. 11:2, 3
3) Matt. 18:1–4
4) Luke 9:46–48
5) 1 Cor. 5:6–8
6) 2 Cor. 2:17
7) 2 Cor. 1:12
8) 1 Pet. 2:1–3
9) 2 Cor. 1:12; 11:13
10) 2 Cor. 6:11–13

85.   *Sin*

Let us never say, God, that we have not sinned
or we make you a liar and your word is not in us.[1]

~

Rather we present ourselves as slaves of obedience
which leads us to righteousness,
not of that which leads us to death.[2]

~

We are set free from sin and are bound to your service.
Deepen this freedom within us
and strengthen our commitment.[3]

~

We have met Jesus – encountered the Christ,
may we never refuse to believe in him.[4]

~

Our former self was crucified with Christ
and through this dying we are freed from sin.[5]

~

Help all to believe the message of Jesus
that everyone may have eternal life.[6]

~

Not letting sin reign over our bodies,
making them instruments of evil.[7]

~

We have already died to sin
so how could we go on living in it?[8]

Make our world free with the freedom of your Son.
Then we will be free indeed.[9]

~

Rescue us, God, from the body of this death
as we give thanks to you through Jesus.[10]

REFERENCES
1) 1 John 1:10
2) Rom. 6:16
3) Rom. 6:22
4) John 16:8, 9
5) Rom. 6:6, 7
6) John 3:36
7) Rom. 6:12, 13
8) Rom. 6:1, 2
9) John 8:34–36
10) Rom. 7:22–25

86.   *Social Justice*

'Blessed are those who hunger and thirst for
     righteousness;
they will be filled.'[1]
~

We remember that you, God, have chosen the poor to be
     rich in faith.
May we never dishonour them.[2]
~

Deepen in us our love for our neighbour
as we carry out the works that accompany faith.[3]
~

As believers in Jesus let us not make distinctions
nor with evil thoughts become judges over others.[4]
~

Give us the wisdom, pure, from above,
without trace of partiality – peaceable, gentle.[5]
~

Help us to bring forth a harvest of righteousness,
sown in peace by those who make peace.[6]
~

Let us not set our hearts on silver and gold,
living in luxury and pleasure
but aim at justice in our dealings with others,
not greed at their expense.[7]
~

Call us anew, God, to the making of peace.
Blessed are the peacemakers, your children.[8]

~

Show us your strength and scatter our pride.
Convert our power into lowliness.[9]

~

Let us boast in our lowliness, of being raised up.
Make generous all of our giving.[10]

REFERENCES
1) Matt. 5:6
2) Jas 2:5, 6
3) Jas 2:15–17
4) Jas 2:1–4
5) Jas 3:17
6) Jas 3:18
7) Jas 5:1–6
8) Matt. 5:9
9) Luke 1:52
10) Jas 1:9–11

87. *Suffering*

God, the sufferings of your Son overflow into our lives.
So too does the encouragement we receive through him.[1]

~

Make us happy to suffer for others,
uniting our pain with the passion of Jesus.[2]

~

Our suffering lasts but a little while;
your power, God, endures forever.[3]

~

To suffer for being Christian is no cause for shame
but rather thankfulness for bearing his name.[4]

~

It is a privilege to believe and to suffer for Christ.
God, make us strong in endurance, in faith.[5]

~

For everything else can be counted as loss,
if we really know Christ Jesus, your Son.[6]

~

Mould us through suffering, into the pattern of
     his death.
May we come to know the power of his rising.[7]

~

Strengthen us, God, with the strength of Christ,
sharing with one another the hardships of life.[8]

~

As children of God and joint heirs with Christ,
we share his suffering and also his glory.[9]

~

Give us the courage to die with Jesus,
then we shall live forever with him.[10]

REFERENCES

1) 2 Cor. 1:5
2) Col. 1:24
3) 1 Pet. 5:10, 11
4) 1 Pet. 4:16
5) Phil. 1:29, 30
6) Phil. 3:8–10
7) Phil. 3:8–10
8) Phil. 4:13
9) Rom. 8:16, 17
10) 2 Tim. 2:11, 12

88. *Temptation*

We pray, God, that we may be rooted in faith
and not fall away in times of testing.[1]
~

Your Son Jesus was tempted by what he suffered.
Jesus, help those who are now being tested.[2]
~

Just as we share in the sufferings of Christ,
we will shout for joy when his glory is revealed.[3]
~

Keep us, God, from the hour of trial.
May we keep your word of patient endurance.[4]
~

Approaching with boldness your throne of grace
to receive mercy and grace in our time of need.[5]
~

Let us not use our power for self-indulgence
nor tempt our God to prove ourselves.
Following not evil to gain worldly power
– away with such things – we worship you, God.[6]
~

Protect us with your power as we suffer various trials.
Make genuine our faith – more precious than gold.
Bring it to praise and glory.[7]
~

Strengthen our endurance when faith is tested.
Bring us to maturity and completeness
    – lacking in nothing.[8]

~

When our mission, with its temptations to give up,
    is ended,
may we bow our head and give up our spirit,
praying with Jesus: 'It is finished.'[9]

REFERENCES
1) Luke 8:11–15
2) Heb. 2:18
3) 1 Pet. 4:12, 13
4) Rev. 3:10–12
5) Heb. 4:15, 16
6) Matt. 4:1–11
7) 1 Pet. 1:3–7
8) Jas 1:2–4
9) John 19:30

89. *Trinity*

Yes, Father, you love the Son,
and you show him all that you are doing.[1]

~

For in the beginning was the Word
and the Word was with you.[2]

~

You loved him in the Spirit,
before the foundation of the world.
He is the reflection of your own glory
and the exact imprint of your very being.[3]

~

The Son who shared in the glory of your presence
before ever the world began[4]
– the only Son who is close to your heart –
he alone sees you and makes you known.[5]

~

He is the beloved Son
with whom you are well pleased.[6]

~

You know the Son and the Son knows you
and all that you have is his.[7]

~

Yes, God, through the Spirit you love the Son
and through his Spirit, your love is in us.[8]

~

With the Spirit of love, a community of love,
three persons in love,
you, God, are love.[9]

REFERENCES

1) John 5:20
3) John 17:24; Heb. 1:3
5) John 1:18; 17:26
7) John 10:15; 17:10
9) 1 John 4:8

2) John 1:1
4) John 17:5
6) Mark 1:11
8) John 3:35; 17:26

90. *Truth*

Your Word, God, became flesh and lived among us
– full of grace and truth.[1]

~

Help us to speak the truth in love
that we may grow up in every way into Christ.[2]

~

May we never turn away from listening to the truth,
wandering away to myths[3]
but live as your children – children of the light –
fruitful in all that is good, true and right.[4]

~

Bring to our minds what we learned from Christ.
The Spirit is the truth.
The truth is in Jesus.[5]

~

Spirit of God, guide us into all truth.
Declare to us also the things that are to come.[6]

~

If we continue in the word of Jesus,
we will be truly his disciples.
We will learn the truth and the truth will make us free.[7]

~

Gift each heart with a love for the truth,
for refusing to love truth is to perish.[8]

~

Jesus is the way, the truth, and the life.
Sanctify us, God, in the truth.[9]

~

With Jesus who was born and came into the world,
let us always testify to the truth.[10]

REFERENCES
1) John 1:14   2) Eph. 4:15
3) 2 Tim. 4:3, 4   4) Eph. 5:8, 9
5) Eph. 4:19–21; 1 John 5:6   6) John 16:13
7) John 8:31, 32   8) 2 Thess. 2:9, 10
9) John 14:6; 17:19   10) John 18:37

91. *Union with God*

We thank you, God, for birthing us anew
through water and the Spirit.[1]

~

Give us the water that springs forth within,
gushing up to life eternal.[2]

~

Help us to worship in spirit and in truth,
for you yourself are spirit.[3]

~

Strengthen our faith in the One you have sent.
May his word abide in us.[4]

~

Give to all a believer's heart.
Rivers of living water shall flow.[5]

~

You abide with us, God; you are within us.
Deepen our knowing – our awareness.[6]

~

Jesus is the vine and we the branches.
Nurture our faith in his abiding presence.[7]

~

May the Spirit guide us into all the truth
and your love be poured into our hearts.[8]

~

Protect us in your name, our God.
That, as Jesus prayed, we may be one.[9]

~

You will see us again and our hearts will rejoice
– a joy that can never be taken.[10]

REFERENCES
1) John 3:3–7
2) John 4:14
3) John 4:24
4) John 5:37, 38
5) John 7:37–39
6) John 14:19, 20
7) John 15:4, 5
8) John 16:12–14; Rom. 5:5
9) John 17:11
10) John 16:22

92. *Victory*

With Jesus, we lift up our eyes to God
and give thanks for the hearing of our prayer.
We know God hears us always.[1]

~

Thanks to God for our faith, through Jesus,
enabling our loving of all God's people,
because of the hope stored up for us in heaven.[2]

~

May the peace of Christ reign in our hearts
for this is our calling as one,[3]
joyful at all times, constant in prayer.
This is your plan, God, for us, in Christ Jesus.[4]

~

From the riches of your glory, you fulfil all our needs.
To you is glory forever.[5]

~

For we know that whatever is born of God,
this conquers the world[6]
and we believe in Jesus the Son.
Our faith conquers the world.[7]

~

When our bodies put on immortality,
death too will be swallowed up in victory
and then we can say 'Where is your sting?
Where is your victory, O death?'[8]

Sanctify us, God, and keep us blameless.
You are the One who is faithful.[9]

~

Thanks to you for giving us the victory
through Jesus Christ, our Saviour.[10]

REFERENCES

1) John 11: 41, 42
2) Col. 1:3–5
3) Col. 3:15
4) 1 Thess. 5:16–18
5) Phil. 4:19
6) 1 John 5:4
7) 1 John 5:5
8) 1 Cor. 15:52–56
9) 1 Thess. 5:23, 24
10) 1 Cor. 15:57

93.   *Waiting*

As we wait for adoption,
the redemption of our bodies,
gift us anew, God, with the fruit of your Spirit.[1]

~

With inward groaning and through the spirit of faith,
we eagerly wait for the hope of righteousness.[2]

~

Help us bear fruit with patient endurance,
holding fast to the word with honesty and goodness.[3]

~

Like Simeon looking forward to Israel's consolation,
strengthen our waiting, deepen our hope.[4]

~

Mould our lives into holiness and godliness
as we wait for and hasten the coming of your day.[5]

~

When we meet persecution,
when troubles arise,
enable our waiting, make strong our endurance.[6]

~

Ready us to wait like the Baptist, John.
We know you will come when we least expect.[7]

~

To those who experience the pain of waiting,
let us try to show the compassion of Jesus.[8]

With the testimony of Christ strengthened among us,
we await the revealing of Jesus, your Son.[9]

~

Like the apostles, in unity and prayer-filled hope,
let us wait for the fulfilment of promise.[10]

REFERENCES
1) Rom. 8:22, 23   2) Gal. 5:5
3) Luke 8:15   4) Luke 2:29–32
5) 2 Pet. 3:11, 12   6) Mark 4:17
7) Matt. 11:3; 24:50   8) Mark 8:2
9) 1 Cor. 1:6, 7   10) Acts 1:4

94. *Water*

God, through the guiding power of your spirit
lead us to springs of the water of life.[1]

~

Give to us this water in abundance.
We who are thirsty wish to come.[2]

~

The water you give will become a spring
gushing up to eternal life.[3]

~

Help us to believe in Jesus more deeply.
Whoever believes will never be thirsty.[4]

~

Gift every person with a believer's heart.
Rivers of living water shall flow.[5]

~

Cleanse our world and touch it with healing.
Make us generous in reaching out.[6]

~

Jesus, you used water for the first of your signs,
revealing your glory while meeting a need.[7]

~

Like a slave, you washed the apostles' feet,
showing with water, God's love for us all.[8]

~

Be with us as we walk over the waters of life.
Let us hear your words: 'It is I, take heart.'[9]

~

Water of life, God, bright as crystal,
flowing from your throne and the throne of the Lamb.[10]

REFERENCES

1) Rev. 7:17   2) Rev. 22:17
3) John 4:14   4) John 6:35
5) John 7:37–39   6) John 5:6–9
7) John 2:1–11   8) John 13:3–5
9) Mark 6:47–52   10) Rev. 22:1

95. *Weakness*

God, we know that our flesh is weak
but our spirit indeed is willing.[1]

~

Help us to accept our own limitations.
You choose what is weak to shame the strong.[2]

~

Jesus, your Son, was crucified in weakness
but lives by your power, the power of God.[3]

~

You will always provide sufficient of your grace
for power is made perfect in weakness.
Let us boast of our weaknesses, knowing contentment,
for when we are weak then we are strong.[4]

~

Ready us to welcome those weak in faith
putting up with their failings, not pleasing ourselves.[5]

~

For at the right time, when we were still weak,
your son Jesus died for us, the ungodly.[6]

~

For the sake of the gospel, we become weak to the weak,
all things to all people, to win some at least.[7]

~

Your weakness, God, is stronger than our strength;
your foolishness above human wisdom.
We want to know Jesus, the crucified Christ,
knowing his power at work in our weakness.[8]

~

We await with longing the resurrection of the dead
when what is perishable becomes imperishable
and what is sown in weakness is raised in power.[9]

~

Though afflicted but not crushed, perplexed but not
    despairing,
we own that the power belongs to you, God.
Be with us in our weakness.[10]

REFERENCES

1) Matt. 26:41

2) Rom. 6:19; 1 Cor. 1:27

3) 2 Cor. 13:3, 4

4) 2 Cor. 12:7–10

5) Rom. 14:1; 15:1

6) Rom. 5:6

7) 1 Cor. 9:22, 23

8) 1 Cor. 1:20–25

9) 1 Cor. 15:42, 43

10) 2 Cor. 4:7–11

96. *Wisdom*

God, you have made foolish the wisdom of the world;
the world did not know you through wisdom.[1]

~

So we proclaim the gospel, not with eloquence
but the crucified Christ – your power and your wisdom.[2]

~

You have chosen us, God – the foolish in the world,
chosen us in Christ, to shame the wise.[3]

~

May our faith never rest on human wisdom alone
but on the power of your spirit – the spirit of Christ
    Jesus.[4]

~

Open our hearts ever more deeply,
as we speak in words not humanly taught
but taught by your Spirit to those who are spiritual.[5]

~

Prepare us to become fools that we may become wise,
for the wisdom of this world is foolishness to you.[6]

~

Gift us with grace and godly sincerity
that earthly wisdom may not be our boast.[7]

~

In all spiritual wisdom and understanding, God,
fill us with the knowledge of your will
that we may lead lives worthy of you,
bearing fruit in every good work.[8]

~

Keep us from envy and selfish ambition.
Grace us with gentleness, born of wisdom.[9]

~

We confess our lacking in wisdom, God,
but in faith, never doubting, we ask you to fill us.[10]

REFERENCES
1) 2) 3) 1 Cor. 1:17–31   4) 5) 1 Cor. 2:6–13
6) 1 Cor. 3:18–20   7) 2 Cor. 1:12
8) Col. 1:9, 10   9) Jas 3:13–15
10) Jas 1:5, 6

97.   *Witness*

And a voice from heaven said:
'This is my Son, the beloved, with whom I am
   well pleased.'[1]

~

Yes, God, the work that Jesus did testified that you had
   sent him.
Be with us in our mission as we witness to the truth.[2]

~

Your Spirit is the one that testifies.
We know the Spirit is truth.[3]

~

Nourish in our hearts the faith you have given
– eternal life in Jesus, your Son.[4]

~

Jesus, you are the faithful witness, the origin of
   God's creation.
For this you were born and came into the world
to testify to the truth.[5]

~

Like those who witnessed Christ's death and his rising,
let us, God, be witnesses to all in our world[6]
by the word of our testimony, even to death,
and in the power of your spirit,
by the blood of the Lamb.[7]

~

With John, let us testify to Jesus, the light.
He enlightens the heart of all who receive him.[8]

~

Thank you, God, for the gift of the scriptures,
testifying to Jesus and giving us life.[9]

~

That all may have fellowship with you and your Son,
let us testify to the Word that all may be one.[10]

REFERENCES

1) Matt. 3:17
3) 1 John 5:6
5) Rev. 1:4, 5; 3:14; John 18:37
7) Rev. 12:11; Acts 1:8
9) John 5:39

2) John 5:36
3) 1 John 5:10, 11
6) Luke 24:46, 47; Acts 22:14, 15
8) John 1:6–9
10) 1 John 1:1–4

98.   *Woman*

God, when the fullness of time had come,
you sent your Son, born of a woman.¹

~

Truly, Mary is blessed among women
and blessed is the fruit of her womb.²

~

Like Elizabeth, gift mothers with the fullness of
    your spirit.
Let the child within them leap for joy.³

~

With Anna the prophet, let us speak about Jesus.
Deepen our spirit of prayer and fasting.⁴

~

Bring us willingly to share of our plenty,
remembering the poor widow who offered her all.⁵

~

May we sit at the feet of Jesus, like Mary,
listening to him in the home of our heart.⁶

~

As sinners, knowing deeply the joy of forgiveness,
make us great, God, in showing our love.⁷

~

Give us the faith of the Canaanite woman
who trusted totally when all seemed lost.⁸

~

And gift us with grace and tender compassion,
like the women on Calvary – loyal to the end.[9]

REFERENCES
1) Gal. 4:4
2) Luke 1:42
3) Luke 1:41, 42
4) Luke 2:36–38
5) Mark 12:41–44
6) Luke 10:38–42
7) Luke 7:36–50
8) Matt. 15:21–28
9) Matt. 27:55–61

99. The Word

'In the beginning was the Word
and the Word was with God and the Word was God.'[1]

~

'And the Word became flesh
and lived among us.'
Let us proclaim what we have seen and heard
concerning the Word of life.[2]

~

God, your Word is truth.
Cleanse us by the Word
and sanctify us in the truth.[3]

~

Give us grace to keep your word
and then we shall never see death.
Deepen our love and make us faithful.
Your words are spirit and life.[4]

~

Jesus, you spoke as God commanded you.
May everyone believe in the word.[5]

~

With Peter, we ask 'To whom can we go?
You have the words of eternal life.'[6]

~

May we always remember your death and your rising,
the scripture and the word that you have spoken.[7]

Fill our hearts, God, with total acceptance
and a deep understanding of your word.[8]

~

Gift us with ready obedience to your word
that your love in us may reach perfection.
In you we abide.
Let us walk like Jesus.
We want to be found in him.[9]

REFERENCES
1) John 1:1
3) John 15:3; 17:17
5) John 12:48–50; 4:41
7) John 2:22
9) 1 John 2:5, 6

2) John 1:14; 1 John 1:3
4) John 8:51; 14:24; 6:63
6) John 6:68
8) John 8:43

100. *Worship*

Let us worship our God in spirit and in truth.
The time for true worship is here.[1]
You seek us, God, to worship thus
for you are spirit and truth.[2]

~

Draw our hearts ever closer to you
that we may worship in sincerity and faith.[3]

~

Make yourself known to all in our world.
Help us in proclaiming your word.[4]

~

You made the world and everything in it.
You are the God of heaven and earth.[5]

~

Depending not on our work or service
for you give life and breath to all things.[6]

~

With conscience clear we worship our God,
remembering all people in prayer, day and night.[7]

~

In faith let us turn to the law and the prophets
worshipping always the God of our ancestors.[8]

~

With the joy of the women on Easter morn
may we fall at the feet of Jesus in worship.[9]

And when we are called to the mountain-top
let us worship in total, unquestioning faith.[10]

REFERENCES
1) John 4:23, 24   2) John 4:23, 24
3) Matt. 15:7–9   4) 5) 6) Acts 17:23–25
7) 2 Tim. 1:3   8) Acts 24:14
9) Matt. 28:9   10) Matt. 28:16, 17